Break the Chains of
TRANSGENERATIONAL PARENTING

*And Learn How to
Re-Parent Yourself*

DOROTHY HUSEN, LMFT

Copyright © 2024 by Dorothy Husen
All rights reserved.

No part of this publication may be reproduced, stored in a retrieval system, or transmitted in any form or by any means, electronic, mechanical, photocopying, recording, scanning, or otherwise, without the prior written permission of the author.

Limit of Liability/Disclaimer of Warranty: While the publisher and author have used their best efforts in preparing this book, they make no representations or warranties with respect to the accuracy or completeness of the contents of this book and specifically disclaim any implied warranties of merchantability or fitness for a particular purpose. No warranty may be created or extended by sales representatives or written sales materials. The advice and strategies contained herein may not be suitable for your situation. You should consult with a professional when appropriate. Neither the publisher nor the author shall be liable for any loss of profit or any other commercial damages, including but not limited to special, incidental, consequential, personal, or other damages.

The stories related in the book from the author's own life are true. However, when it comes to client stories, in order to protect their privacy, the author has used amalgamations of cases to illustrate points. She has also changed names and details in all client stories.

BREAK THE CHAINS OF TRANSGENERATIONAL PARENTING
And Learn How to Re-Parent Yourself

by Dorothy Husen, LMFT

PSY044000 **PSYCHOLOGY** / Developmental / Lifespan Development
SEL024000 **SELF-HELP** / Self-Management / Stress Management
FAM034000 **FAMILY & RELATIONSHIPS** / Parenting / General

ISBN: 979-8-88636-046-2 (paperback)
ISBN: 979-8-88636-047-9 (ebook)

Cover design by Clare Finney

Printed in the United States of America

Authority Publishing
13389 Folsom Blvd #300-256
Folsom, CA 95630
800-877-1097
www.AuthorityPublishing.com

Dedication

For my grandchildren, Elena Grace and John Mabon.

TABLE OF CONTENTS

Introduction   *vii*

1 – The Fear Loop   *1*

2 – The Truth of You   *15*

3 – Your Inner-Child   *25*

4 – Re-parenting Yourself   *35*

5 – Re-Parenting Your Inner-Infant (Ages 0-1)   *47*

6 – Re-Parenting Your Inner-Toddler (Ages 2-4)   *61*

7 – Re-Parenting Your Inner-Small-Child (Ages 4-7)   *75*

8 – From Make-Believe to Reality (Ages 8-11)   *91*

9 – Your Inner-Tween (Ages 10-13)   *105*

10 – Your Inner-Adolescent (Ages 14-26)   *121*

11 – Re-Parenting: A Job that Never Ends   *135*

Acknowledgments   *145*

Notes   *147*

Introduction

Years ago, while studying to become a marriage and family therapist, I was introduced to the Circle of Security. Developed by psychotherapists Kent Hoffman, Glen Cooper, and Bert Powell in their clinic in Spokane, Washington, the circle is a visual representation of how attachment works between parents and children—and why the quality of that attachment is so important. At the top of the circle are the parents' hands, signifying both a "secure base" from which a child cultivates the self-assurance necessary to move around the circle (explore their world) and a "safe haven" to which a child can return whenever they need to refill their emotional cup, to be understood, encouraged, and assured. The more a child experiences both the base and the haven as reliable and supportive, the more self-confidence the child develops and the freer they feel to investigate the world. This freedom that grows from a foundation of security protects them from being overly swayed by outside influences, enabling them to develop into the unique individuals they were meant to be. When children don't have the benefit of a secure base or dependable haven at the top of the circle, they move out onto the circle (the world) without the benefit of a solid sense of self, belonging, or inherent worth—making navigating the world and finding their place in it difficult, confusing, and scary. More often than not, they find themselves off track.

LIFE AT THE BOTTOM

Many years after that first encounter with the Circle of Security and now a practicing therapist myself, I was preparing to use the circle for a parenting group I was coaching. As I pulled the illustration up on my screen, I found myself staring at the bottom of the circle—when the child is farthest away from "the hands" and most outwardly focused as they look to make sense of the world and themselves. In that moment, I realized I'd spent most of my life at the bottom of the Circle of Security looking outside myself for the answers and guidance I needed.

For a multitude of reasons explored in later chapters, as a child, I—like many children—hadn't experienced much of what was supposed to happen at the top of the circle. Though I had two parents at home, my secure parental base from which to develop self-worth and self-confidence hadn't been all that reliable. My parents—both survivors of World War II—were dealing (or not dealing) with their own issues. So my focus turned outward. I depended on sources outside myself to tell me how to be in the world. Through those borrowed lenses, my interpretations of my experiences (how the world worked and who I was) weren't always on target—especially when infant-me, child-me, and teen-me were doing the interpreting. Yet, these misconceptions were all I knew and so they became my truth. And because they were never questioned—I didn't know to question them—they set the patterns of my thinking and behavior. They followed me throughout my development and into adulthood, influencing my decision-making, what I thought of myself, and what I thought was possible for someone like me.

The truth is that none of us moves around that circle without creating and incorporating into our thought processes some misbeliefs about the world and about ourselves. For instance, most of us allow the labels parents, teachers, or other adults stick us with as children—"the smart one," "the pretty one," "the athletic one," or whatever—to continue as part of our adult identities. Those who suffer trauma in childhood—such as assault, the death of a parent, abandonment, chronic illness, or some other tragedy—often form conclusions about the event using the limited cognitive abilities and life experience they had when it happened—i.e., child logic. Even children who experience a secure attachment to their parents, develop a strong sense of self, and receive understanding and guidance at every turn can still hold onto a few misbeliefs formed in childhood that trip them up in their adult lives.

Because they are all we know, these misbeliefs become "facts" to us. We then build our thought process and behavior patterns on these "facts"—using them to manage (or mismanage) our adult lives. The result being that no matter where life takes us or what outward changes we make in our relationships, our careers, or our goals, we always seem to find ourselves facing the same obstacles, having the same arguments, and with things not working out once again.

FINDING INWARD

It wouldn't be until I found therapy—or if I'm being honest, therapy found me (which again, we'll get into later)—that I came to understand the connection between how I thought about what happened to me in my childhood and how my adult life was playing out. I had become who others thought I should be. Through a therapeutic technique called "re-parenting," I discovered I could trace the foundations of my most potential-limiting thought and behavior patterns in adulthood to the childhood events I'd formed misbeliefs around. By questioning and more importantly, coming to a deep understanding of the conclusions I made as a child about life experiences, I could both change my patterns and heal my childhood wounds.

In my learning to "re-parent" myself, I learned to turn my focus inward, toward the misinformed child within me. By becoming curious about what I thought I knew, I was able to question those foundational misbeliefs, process them with an adult perspective, and find a more accurate and mature truth for myself. Finally, I could see with compassion what I'd been through as a child, how it had shaped me, and who I wanted to be moving forward. Through that inward lens, so many of the beliefs (really misbeliefs) that had determined my world and my opinion of myself for my whole life fell apart. Without outside distortion, who I was and am got clearer for me; understanding and self-love found room to flourish.

As my self-exploration deepened, I identified patterns driven by fears that were dictating my behaviors and decisions, and keeping me from being myself. I was able to see my life more honestly and thoughtfully. In time, I exposed the foundations of my fears for the fallacy they were. No longer afraid or ashamed, I became free to make choices that would lead to a life I wanted and the connection to other people I craved. I became my secure base and safe haven—my own hands at the top of the circle. Now instead of looking outside myself for life instructions and validation, I looked inside myself to know what I valued and let those values guide me. From that healthy place, I was able to recognize and thus avoid negatively patterned thoughts and behaviors, and move forward in my life as a full-fledged adult in control of my life for the first time.

CHANGING FOCUS

In my own therapy practice, I noticed so many clients were also stuck in thought and behavior patterns that were getting in the way of what they wanted for their lives and sometimes causing depression and chronic illness. Of course, they didn't see it that way, not at first. Their interpretation of themselves and the world around them seemed normal and accurate to them because that's all they knew and had ever known. It's the proverbial fish in water. I understood because that's where I'd been too.

For clients who were open to it, I began teaching them to re-parent themselves. The re-parenting process I designed for my practice goes beyond the conventional talk therapy (cognitive behavioral therapy) I received. It incorporates information on child development, as well as mind-body therapeutic techniques. I found these additions help clients get to the root causes of their issues in a more efficient and straightforward manner. In time, they become adept at re-parenting themselves without my guidance, whenever needed.

INSIDE THIS BOOK

I wrote this book to chronicle my re-parenting journey and how the process has worked for my clients in my practice. I wanted to document—to get down in black and white—how "re-parenting" has changed the trajectory of so many lives for the better. And how it can do the same for you. In these chapters, my hope is that you, the reader, see how re-parenting works, who it helps best, and how you might use it to examine and relieve the challenges in your life today—and once you learn it, for the rest of your life.

The first few chapters explain how we form misbeliefs in childhood and become trapped by them throughout adulthood. Illustrations from my life as well as stories based on clients' lives help readers see how our childhood misbeliefs express themselves and cause havoc in our lives—distorting our ability to understand our current situation, warping our decision-making, and preventing us from moving forward in life in myriad ways.

Chapter 3 introduces you to your inner-child—taking the "woo" out of this term and explaining what an inner-child is, that we all have them, and how to recognize yours. Chapters 4 and 5 then provide an overview of the re-parenting process itself, as well as the terms and tools you'll want to familiarize yourself with as you read more about re-parenting in action.

The next several chapters—Chapters 6 through 10—take you developmental phase by developmental phase showing what re-parenting looks like from inner-infant to inner-adolescent. You learn how your child-brain functioned at every age, what motivated you, and what issues you were most likely to misinterpret at that stage in life. You see how the misbeliefs of each phase typically manifest in adulthood, giving you a guide as to which inner-child might hold the keys to a persistent issue in your life. Most important, you come to understand what your inner-child at each developmental phase might need from adult-you now, so you know better how to approach and re-parent that inner-child.

The book's final chapter offers the support you'll need—as well as a few tips—if you choose to put the re-parenting process to work in your own life. To ease your way, it also provides an acronym—P.A.R.E.N.T.—that I developed and use in my own practice to make it easier for clients to remember the steps to re-parenting whenever they need them.

Each chapter ends with an exercise to help you absorb the information discussed in that chapter and to give you a foundation from which to start your own re-parenting journey, uncover some misbeliefs, and reacquaint yourself with your inner-child. I suggest you read the book straight through once to give you a good idea of the process—and then move through the chapters more slowly, working through the exercises as you go.

Please note that the stories I relate in the book from my own life are true. However, to protect my clients, I've used amalgamations of cases to illustrate points. I've also changed names and details in all client stories.

FULL CIRCLE

Inside all of us is the knowledge of what's true for us and what we need to be who we are and realize our full potential in life. Most of us just need some help to bring that self-knowledge back into our consciousness. Re-parenting teaches you to take your mental and physical pain for the signs they are, to pay attention to them, and to follow them where they lead you. Through re-parenting, you can correct the misbeliefs that hide your true nature, relieve the fears that keep you playing small, and heal the wounds that have kept you in shame. Re-parenting puts you at the top of your Circle of Security—where you become your own secure base and safe haven, giving your inner-children and yourself unconditional love and dependable support. Re-parenting sets your life on a course of radical self-acceptance and self-love that allows you to live this life—not full of judgment as a test—but with curiosity for the adventure it is. That's been my experience and the experience of hundreds of my clients. My hope is that it becomes your experience, too.

1

THE FEAR LOOP

I remember my mom's face flushed red and eyes wide with anger as she searched the kitchen drawers for the wooden spoon. She growled how my four-year-old brother was going to get it, how she had to beat the rebellion out of him.

This was a regular occurrence at my house. At eight years old, I felt scared for myself. I didn't want to get hit. I felt angry at my brother for disobeying my mother once again. I felt sorry for my mom because she had to deal with a rebellious, disobedient child like my brother. He was "bad."

That is what I believed.

Of course, he wasn't bad. No child is bad—especially not at four years old. But how could I know that? At eight, all I knew is what my parents showed me and told me. And based on their words and actions—especially my mother's—my brother was bad. I decided I wasn't going to be like my brother. I was going to be "good." This would please my mother. She wouldn't have to beat the rebellion out of me. I even aligned with my mother's anger toward my brother, so she would see me as her ally.

It worked. I became the "good" one in our family—which I believed would save me from the pain of punishment.

School reinforced what I'd experienced at home. Mrs. Page, my second- and third-grade teacher, was old and wrinkly with gray hair. She had bony fingers and skin that sagged around her arms. Her face would turn red and her eyes would bug out right before she grabbed a misbehaving student, usually a boy. She'd dig her fingernails into his tender arm flesh and shake, shake, shake him back and forth, as she screamed into his face to shut up and be quiet when she was talking.

I also remember the paddle that hung in our principal's office—it had words carved in it alluding to bad kids. It hung where everyone could see it. On occasion, we'd hear whack, whack, whack coming from the office, followed by a child crying.

From home to school, what I remember most was feeling scared. Always scared. Every minute, I figured I was one mistake away from getting it with the wooden spoon, the nail-digging shakes, or the huge paddle.

Through these early experiences—limited as they were—I internalized a deep belief that bad children would be punished, so I needed to obey and be good or harm would come to me. As I grew, far from leaving me, this belief guided me. It was always in the back of my head, warning me and causing me to focus all my attention and energy—not on my own development—but on pleasing whatever adult or authority figure I was with.

More than four decades and a lot of personal damage later, I would come to know this as my fear loop—a thought pattern, motivated by a belief (or misbelief) that drives our behavior, shapes our personality, and constructs negative patterns in our lives that prevent us from developing our full potential.

If you are feeling stuck in life right now—making choices that seem to consistently send you in the wrong direction and land you in the same place, facing the same challenges and frustrations over and over again—you, too, are likely caught in a fear loop. You, too, may be motivated by beliefs set in your mind long ago (beliefs you may not even be aware of and may no longer be true) that now keep you from seeing the reality of your situation, from knowing yourself, and from living the life you want.

WHERE BELIEFS COME FROM

Like I did, all human beings learn who we are and gain a sense of ourselves from our parents or caregivers. From the moment we're born, we look to how our parents act and react to us—how they nurture and care for us—to gauge how to think about ourselves. We observe their behaviors and listen to their tone of voice to know what is good and what is bad, safe and unsafe, and what pleases them or makes them angry. With this knowledge, we intuitively pick up how we fit into our family, and we start to form our own beliefs about who we are and how the world works.

We take those beliefs out into the world with us. At school, we use them to determine where we belong among our peers and what we are capable of (or not). They guide us in what to study, what to try, who to befriend, and how to befriend. They set the bar for our judging others and ourselves. As we grow, our beliefs become the assumptions we use to navigate our lives, to make our choices, to manage our relationships and our problems.

Most of us go through our entire lives assuming how our parents viewed the world—and more significantly, how they viewed us—is right. But if our parents' beliefs were defective to begin with or no longer true—if they were misbeliefs—and we incorporated them into our worldview without question, they can become an invisible force, further fortified by our life choices, that catches us up in a fear loop.

THE POWER OF MISBELIEF

During the pandemic, like many people, I moved my business—a psychotherapy practice—to my home. And like many, I used this opportunity to renovate my home office, applying the principles of feng shui to ensure a peaceful energy.

One morning, after tapping into that energy and getting in the flow,

I needed more coffee. As I opened the door to the hallway, my sense of peace evaporated. "What's on the carpet?" I bent down to get a closer look and saw little black chunks of something on top of the brand-new white pile. It looked like bits of dirt. "How did Jim (my husband) track that in without me noticing?" I picked up a few of the bits, held them in my hand to examine them. Then, I threw them in the trash, deciding I'd vacuum later. I wanted to get back to work, back to my beautiful office, back to the flow.

An hour or so later, I got up from my desk again, and... "What? Black bits on my office carpet! When had Jim done this?" It was weird. Once again, I picked up the bits, threw them in the trash, and walked toward the bathroom. When I came out, there were more bits glaring up at me.

"Oh, my god! How did I miss these?" Shaking my head in judgment, I imagined Jim walking around the house with a big blob of gooey something attached to his shoe without realizing it. Sighing heavily and rehearsing what I'd say to him as soon as I saw him, I bent down, picked up the bits, and threw them in the trash. As I turned to walk back to my desk, I found more bits on the carpet. "I was right," I said to myself out loud this time. "He's tracked them everywhere." And for the fourth time, I picked them up.

I expected to see a completely clean carpet as I turned around. Instead, it seemed I'd "missed" a few. It was only then, as I bent down for the fifth time that morning to pick the dirt out of my carpet, that I began to question my explanation of events. "Hadn't I just cleaned here? How could I have missed these bits?" And finally, "Where are they coming from?"

With that question, it hit me: "No, could it be? My shoes?" Slowly, with caution, I looked at the soles of my shoes. I stood there for a moment in silence, staring at my discovery. Indeed, my shoes were crumbling, leaving little black bits everywhere I walked. I immediately felt guilty for blaming my husband. Then I had to laugh. I imagined myself in a comedy sketch moving forward picking up bits of rubber while simultaneously dropping bits of rubber behind me.

Even before I picked up my first black bit, it should have been obvious to me that Jim couldn't have tracked dirt into the hallway or my office. For one, I would have seen him. Also—and I knew this while I was simultaneously holding him responsible—Jim wasn't home that morning.

So why had I insisted on blaming Jim, despite mountains of evidence to the contrary? The power of belief.

For years and years whenever I found dirt on the floor, the culprit had always been the shoes, boots, skateboards, bikes, or whatever of one of our two children or Jim tracked in. Over time, my brain learned that it could with certainty associate dirt on the floor with one of them—not me (though now I'm wondering if sometimes it might have been me). So whenever I saw dirt, my brain didn't think about what may have happened. It didn't look for facts or evidence. No. It automatically assigned the fault to one of them—no questions asked, no other avenues explored. With that automatic response, my learned experience solidified into a belief. And since our children were grown and out of the house, my belief could only conclude that Jim tracked in the dirt.

That power of our beliefs can be seen everywhere. When you go to the store, you believe everyone will stand in line and wait their turn to check out. When you put a cake in a hot oven, you believe it will bake. When a person you trust agrees to do something for you, you believe they will do it. When a person you don't trust agrees to do something, you believe they won't do it.

If any of the above doesn't happen the way you believe, it confuses you. Your brain rejects the facts at first (all morning in my case). And then your brain goes into overdrive trying to reason a way to hold on to your belief, despite mounting evidence that it might be wrong. Only when your brain becomes exhausted in that pursuit, does it open enough to make room for possibilities outside your belief.

Our brains do this because beliefs are efficient. Beliefs eliminate doubt and purport certainty. They tell us what is right and what is wrong—without our needing to get into the details. They tell us what we like and don't like—before we've tried it. Our beliefs about ourselves tell us who we are and what we can and cannot do.

Our beliefs allow our brains to form opinions, make decisions, and act automatically without having to go to the effort of asking questions or weighing options. Our beliefs give us confidence in our choices and keep us out of perceived trouble. Without these predetermined conclusions, our brains would be so busy deciding how to approach everyday tasks we'd never have the time, energy, or brain capacity to try new things.

While mostly that's good, there is a downside to belief. When our thinking becomes so automatic that we are unable to question it, we become rigid and our lives become limited. We don't try new things. Even more dangerous, we don't allow for changing circumstances or the possibility that we might be wrong about a situation, another person, or about ourselves. Our lives then become directed by misbelief—which is just as powerful because our brains don't know the difference.

That morning in my office, my brain clung to my misbelief. It took five confrontations with the black bits—count them, five—to force my brain to even consider a different explanation, one that made a lot more sense. My misbelief not only made me look foolish, but it also kept me from seeing the truth and solving my problem.

It's one thing when a misbelief causes you to misjudge the source of a dirty carpet. It's quite another when it causes you to misjudge the truth of your life.

LIVING THE FEAR LOOP

My misbelief that I had to be "good" to avoid harm created the fear loop I would operate from as I grew. My decisions, my actions, my relationship with the world would all be in the cause of that misbelief.

Firmly on that loop, I learned to pay close attention to what people liked, didn't like, and what might anger them. As a very young child, I developed a keen sense of what others wanted from me, and I delivered. If I didn't know what to say, I didn't say anything.

My quietness and compliance brought me accolades from authority figures—making life on that fear loop successful from the standpoint of keeping me out of harm's way. In school, I was always the teacher's pet. Teachers used me as an example to other students: "Class, look at Dorothy. See how she listens to instructions. If you paid attention like Dorothy, you'd know what you're supposed to be working on right now." At home, I was my mother's favorite of her four children by far. My mother would say, "Dorothy, you are such a peaceful presence. I feel I can tell you anything."

But living out my misbelief proved to be anything but peaceful. The truth was I was not good, I was fearful. All I wanted out of life was to fly under the radar and avoid trouble. My fear loop kept my focus on what I needed to be to earn the approval of others. Any part of me that was spirited, curious, rebellious, or authentically me had to be stuffed behind my façade of goodness. I developed no goals that were mine alone. No thoughts about what I might want to do. I never developed my own likes or dislikes. I certainly never developed a voice of my own or even a sense of who I was independent of others.

The fear loop didn't allow me to "grow out of" my misbelief or "get over it." It kept me stuck. And over time, it formed my personality. My existence became one of extreme dependence on others—not for food and shelter, but to define me.

At first, I was dependent on my mother to tell me who I was, what to do, and even what to wear. My worldview was whatever she thought it should be. I convinced myself that I liked what she liked. As I grew, I looked to the Christian religion, then to the United States Navy, and then my marriage to give me a role to play and expectations to conform to. I found I fit well and was most comfortable in any authoritarian institution—any place I didn't have to think for myself. Ironically, being so dependent left me vulnerable to abuse by untrustworthy authority figures, as well as my peers, throughout my life.

To me, the saddest of all of this is that the fear loop prevented me from having what I truly deep down wanted—what every human being wants—connection. Throughout my childhood and well into my adulthood, I longed for a friend, a close friend. At the same time, I was scared of people. Scared I'd be exposed. Scared too much would be asked of me and I wouldn't be able to deliver. I worried most that I didn't have much to offer. There was no real me there to befriend.

To the world, I was quiet, shy, and sweet. I was never angry or confrontational. I was cool as a cucumber, a follower, and a background person. When anyone asked me how I was doing, my standard reply was, "I'm good, thanks." In my mind, their question was a ball thrown toward me. I could catch it, throw it back with some truth, and maybe connect. But I always dodged their toss and let their ball hit the wall of that standard, stilted reply.

All the patterns born of my misbeliefs about the world and about myself had negative, long-term effects on my life. The fear I lived with compounded daily into chronic stress, which developed into complex or developmental post-traumatic stress disorder.

My case may be an extreme example of living out a misbelief. But we all do this to some extent. We might think our problem is anxiety, depression, our relationship or lack thereof, anger issues, disordered eating, or (fill in the blank). But these are not our real problems. These are simply the "black bits" we keep having to pick up. The fundamental issue always comes down to a misbelief about ourselves. How we feel about ourselves. How we see ourselves. How we view the world.

When our lives are based on a misbelief, our actions and decisions are based on a falsehood. So it's no wonder that our lives don't tend to work well. The longer we hold on to our misbeliefs, the more we employ them, the more attached and identified with them we become—the harder it becomes for us to recognize when they are taking us in the wrong direction. The harder it becomes to detach ourselves from them.

I certainly was oblivious to the misbelief that drove my behavior and choices for more than four decades. I didn't consciously think every day that I was acting out of fear. In psychological terms, I repressed my fears, along with my misbelief, and pushed them into my subconscious. My every day experience was more like "this is how life works" and "it's just the way things are" and "I like being good and pleasing people." To me, I had a very "normal," if not a lonely, painful, and exhausting existence.

For most of us, unless we are jolted from our patterned thinking and forced to question our underlying beliefs, we are doomed to keep making the same mistakes and finding ourselves in the same place in our career, in our relationships, in our lives. Our fear loops keep us running in circles, going nowhere, and blaming the wrong things for the black bits in our lives.

STEPPING OFF THE FEAR LOOP

I was forty-eight years old when I found myself sitting face to face with a psychotherapist for the first time. Jim had decided that with our children now grown, I needed a vocation and he needed a change. He'd been working himself to death as an attorney for decades. He thought we should become marriage and family therapists. In my heart, I loved the idea of going back to school—a place of rules and set expectations. But I feared and doubted my ability to one day take on the responsibility of clients, let alone running a practice. As usual though, I said nothing, obeyed, and went to school like a "good" person. Attending so many hours of therapy was a course requirement. That's the only reason I was in that therapist's office.

Though she hadn't yet asked me how I was feeling, as I sat down, I preemptively informed her, "I'm good. My life is good. I don't need therapy. I'm just here to learn how this (therapy) works in real life." In my mind, her office was just another classroom where I'd sit and receive instructions on how to become a therapist. What I experienced, however, was something wholly different.

When my therapist asked me questions about my childhood based on the information I'd provided on a standard intake form, I became triggered to the point that I couldn't talk or move. I froze. I froze in space and time, as if someone had pushed the pause button on a video.

No one had ever gone past "I'm good" before. Now, the truth of my life—including several serious traumatic incidents my misbelief had made me vulnerable to—were poking through.

In time, my therapist said, "Dorothy, I think you have post-traumatic stress disorder." Immediately, I felt in my bones what she said was true. For the first time in my life, I felt something different in myself, something real. These sessions had called me into awareness, knocking my beliefs to the side. I saw reality. In the face of this truth, for the first time in my memory, my fear retreated. For a moment, I was me.

It would take a lot more work and a lot more sessions to keep me in the moment. What my therapist would do in those subsequent sessions was re-parenting me—allowing me to revisit my childhood and re-examine my beliefs. When she acknowledged my inner pain, she stood in for my mom all those years ago. But my therapist did not scare me like my mom did. When I looked at her, I expected shame to wash over me. But shame didn't come. By asking me questions and allowing for my answers—instead of telling me what to do or think—my therapist made it possible for me to eventually reframe myself as the authority figure in my life, the one person who could truly keep me safe. This made it possible for me to challenge the foundational beliefs my parents had passed to me. Were they still true? Were they ever true? What is true for me now? It was the start of my thinking for myself, freeing myself from my fear loop, and becoming an independent adult.

It doesn't matter what the problem is if you are looking in the wrong direction for the solution. If your pain is mental, emotional, or relational, the solution won't be found in another person, another job, or another anything. The solution to the majority of our problems lies within us—in what we believe (or misbelieve) about ourselves and about the world we inhabit. The solution, therefore, comes from you.

RE-PARENTING YOURSELF TO WELLNESS
While re-parenting using talk therapy (also known as cognitive behavioral therapy) led to a breakthrough for me, it was a slow process over-

all. Like most clients, I only had access to my therapist once a week for fifty minutes. My fear loops and misbeliefs, however, had access to me 24/7. Often, I found myself without the skills to recognize them and deal with them—keeping me running on the fear loop until my next therapy appointment.

After I was licensed and went into practice as a marriage and family therapist, I continued to learn about and experience various forms of therapy. I came across numerous mind/body psychotherapies. These therapies use physical feelings in our bodies—such as tension and stress—to uncover areas of misalignment in our lives. They then use physical techniques such as breathing and mindfulness to help us release the blockage and bring our minds, bodies, and lives back into alignment.

Combining these mind/body techniques with my knowledge of human development and psychotherapy, I designed a technique to re-parent myself wherever I was, whenever I needed to. Using this technique of re-parenting, I've been able to replace my misbelief with truth, recognize patterned behavior before it starts, and retire my fear loop for good. My traumas no longer trap me or control my life. Recruiting the body into this effort made it so much faster than working with the mind alone.

As adults, it's up to us to jolt ourselves from our misbeliefs and dismantle our fear loops. Re-parenting gives you the tools to do that. It gives you access through the mind and the body to take yourself back to those formative years. It allows you to bring the beliefs that shaped you into your consciousness, examine the truth of them, and dispel any misbeliefs. Re-parenting allows you to find your truth, break negative patterns, and operate from a place of authenticity.

Re-parenting healed me. As I taught this technique to my clients, they found the same results. Within weeks (not years), they were able to re-parent themselves, move forward in their lives, and achieve success and happiness as they defined it. To this day, hundreds of my clients have used re-parenting to help themselves to escape their misbeliefs and fear loops.

In these pages, we will walk together, step by step, through the re-parenting process. You'll soon learn that you do have the power to re-parent yourself. To come out of hiding. To take back your life from misbeliefs planted so long ago. And to enjoy this life, your life. No one can live your life but you. It's time to get started.

TRY THIS: LOOK INWARD

My misbelief about how "good" I was built a wall of protection around me. So too, your misbeliefs have created walls around you. Walls that prevent you from seeing who you really are.

This first exercise is meant to break down those walls a bit—and give you a glimpse at the real you. To re-parent yourself, you must go back in time, back to procedural or intrinsic memories. These subconscious memories are stored in your body. You access them by developing a skill called interoception.

Interoception is the awareness of one's internal state of the body. How does your chest feel? Is your stomach nervous? Does your back hurt? Or feel tight? Or feel hot? Can you move your jaw? Are your shoulders slumped down and in? Can you feel your heart beating? Do you feel pressure or restlessness in your legs?

Here's how to get there:

- Step 1 – Close your eyes.

    With our eyes open, we are scanning our environment for safety. We are looking where to walk safely. We are looking into the faces and movements and behaviors of other people. We use our vision to see outside of our bodies. When you close your eyes, you eliminate that noise and have no choice but to go inward. So find a quiet place, sit comfortably, and close your eyes.

- Step 2 – Slow, deep breathing.

    Take a slow deep breath in your nose. Bring it all the way down into your belly. Open your chest and fill your lungs. Then slowly exhale and release your breath out of your mouth. Continue to breathe this way throughout the exercise.

- Step 3 – Focus on inhaling and exhaling.

    As you continue to breathe deeply, try to sense the tip of your nose. Feel the cool air coming in your nose. Follow your breath down your windpipe into your lungs. Feel your belly push out. Feel the pressure build inside your chest. Follow your breath as you exhale. Feel your shoulders relax. Feel your belly go down. Feel your lungs release warm air as it travels out of your mouth. Repeat with each breath.

- Ste p 4 – Follow your breath in your mind's eye.

    Now using your imagination, watch your breath move inside your body. Notice yourself pulling air from outside of your body into the inside of your body and back out again. As you follow your breath in your mind, your attention will follow and go from outside your body to the inside of your body. Do this for one minute, every day. Notice how it changes your focus and attention.

2

THE TRUTH OF YOU

To many, my mother's use of a wooden spoon to keep order in our house isn't shocking. Just a generation or so ago, spankings were a common part of childhood. As adults, my siblings—my older brother, my older sister, and my younger brother—and I would sit around the family table with my parents listening to the boys cheerfully recount how, as children, they'd hide the wooden spoon from my mother so she couldn't "whack" them. Mom always responded by wagging her finger at her grown sons, pretending to be angry once again. Then my older brother would say, "Yeah, we deserved it. But you had to keep buying new wooden spoons!" And everyone would burst out laughing at the memory.

My husband, Jim—also a child of the second half of the twentieth century—has his own favorite "spanking story." Whenever he did something wrong, he'd get sent to his room to wait for his father to come and spank him. Once while waiting, Jim came up with what he believed to be an ingenious idea: He put on seven pairs of underwear under his jeans to pad the impact. "But my dad was too smart to be fooled by me," Jim always says with a twinkle in his eye. "He quickly caught on to what I'd done. So he whacked me right below my underwear padding." Then, to make sure whoever is listening gets it, Jim runs his finger along his thighs to the exact spot. "See. Right here where it's real tender. Wowee! Owwwuch! Did it hurt! I couldn't sit down for days." And just like when my brothers tell their wooden-spoon story, everyone laughs.

AUTHORITARIAN RULE: WHERE "SHOULDS" COME FROM

Why are these stories funny to us? Partly because, as a society, we once believed hitting to be a productive and acceptable form of disciplining a child. Who among us isn't familiar with the expression "spare the rod, spoil the child." As counterintuitive as it might sound to modern ears, hitting was the way to teach children right from wrong. It was believed that the threat of physical pain would keep them in line, ensure they did as they were told, and keep them from doing dangerous things. We believed spanking was what responsible parents did. (Some people still think this way.)

When taught by this authoritarian model, however, all we learn is to obey a person who has power over us. We learn that doing what they want keeps us safe from their anger, maybe even earns us praise, and *not* doing it can result in punishment, maybe even physical pain. Our beliefs about what's right and what's wrong then come from fear, not understanding.

At its worst, this causes us to choose behaviors simply to avoid punishment or to get praise. We don't develop our own intrinsic motivations, sense of morality, or our own ideas. Our inner moral compass and our values never develop. "Might makes right" becomes our guiding principle, our belief (whether we are conscious of it or not). We become dependent on authorities outside ourselves to tell us what to think, what to do, and who we are. We live our lives striving to do what we "should" do, according to that authority, whether or not it's what we want to do or a good fit for us.

This authoritarian, hierarchal model is how most institutions in our society from the government to religions to the family have historically been structured—and for some good reasons. Human beings weren't long on this earth before they discovered there was safety in numbers. Those who formed a community could share the hard work of surviving, as well as protect each other from predators, the aftermath of natural disasters, and people from outside their community.

To make a community work, however, takes cooperation. Cooperation means decisions must be made and rules created to ensure those decisions are carried out and to keep order among group members. Consequently, punishment is needed to keep people from going against the decisions or breaking the rules—both of which would threaten the group's cohesion and safety. Typically, a leader and ruling class emerge to make decisions and ensure order. Community members sign over their autonomy to this authority in return for the perks of belonging to the group.

As you would expect, the authoritarian model has evolved to favor conformity and strict obedience to authority above personal freedom. Even in societies where kings have been replaced by presidents, prime ministers, and democracy, these authoritarian structures and our inclination to obey them persist. Throughout our culture, you can see obedience to authority celebrated in our art, especially in our stories. The Bible is full of such tales. So is Greek mythology. Even our modern entertainment reinforces the positives of obedience to a good ruler.

For instance, watching Disney's 1994 release *The Lion King,* children learn all about the peace, order, and good life that results from subjecting oneself to authority. The movie opens with the breathtaking scene of the most majestic animals—giraffes, hippos, elephants, and others—crossing the Sub-Saharan African landscape in harmony, no fighting in this group. They are on their way to pay homage to their king, the lion Mufasa, and his newborn son and heir to the throne, Simba. When all are assembled, Rafiki, the shaman, raises Simba for all of Mufasa's subjects to see. The music crescendos and the animals bend their knee in homage to authoritarian rule continuing for another generation. Viewers get the message that authority is good and that all decent, noble, and morally right animals obey and subjugate themselves to it.

But just in case they didn't get it, enter Scar—Mufasa's brother and the movie's villain. He wants to be king—which is outside the rules. And viewers can see for themselves that Scar's insistence on going against the cultural custom has made him want to do terrible things—like kill his baby nephew. It also made everyone hate him. His only friends are ugly hyenas, and they kill him in the end (sorry for the spoiler). By the time Scar meets that end, viewers understand that not only is respecting authority the path to the good life, but those who go against it create all kinds of discord, become outcasts, and meet a bad fate.

The Lion King was a blockbuster movie. It's reportedly made around $11.6 billion to date. That's a lot of little kids who received the pro-authority message. You could argue that it's just a movie. But it's one that promotes authoritarianism, as well as favoritism between siblings. Both of which reinforce the misbelief of unworthiness of someone who doesn't conform, which can take away from a child's potential.

WHAT "SHOULDS" BECOME

It's not that children shouldn't obey their parents or the rules of their culture. It's that we don't want them—or us—to do it without understanding why they should. Children who grow up in an environment where they fear trying because they fear being wrong never figure out who they are and what they can do. They live their lives governed by a list of "shoulds" somebody else—their parents, their teachers, their culture—made up for them.

For the most part, these authorities believe their rules and their set expectations keep children on the right path to a successful life. In reality, demanding strict, unquestioned obedience to any outward authority keeps children down. It teaches them not to trust in themselves. When there is no room for independence, we can't think for ourselves. There is no growth and innovation. Cultures stagnate. People stagnate.

Jim and I were both raised in authoritarian households—with clear rules and even clearer expectations. In both our homes, the focus was on what others thought of us and so keeping up outward appearances. Truth, feelings, and authenticity were not valued; in fact, they weren't even discussed. From early ages, we both knew what we "should" do. And without question and to the best of our ability, we both did it.

Jim's family wanted to be seen as winners. As children, Jim and his two brothers were expected to excel at sports. Jim, however, didn't like sports. He was a sensitive, creative kid. But he pushed the books he loved aside to spend his time playing on various teams. He had to work twice as hard as his brothers, who both were gifted athletes, to earn the same amount of acceptance from his parents.

Adhering to that "should" produced the misbelief in Jim that in order for people to like and accept him, he needed to work hard and be outstanding at whatever he did. Not surprisingly, Jim became a workaholic. And this misbelief became such a part of his worldview that he never questioned the truth of it until he found himself so physically and mentally exhausted in his mid-forties that he feared he was burning out.

As I discussed in Chapter 1, I got the message at a very early age that my mother expected me to be the good girl, the peacemaker. I also learned early on that our church expected me to become a wife and mother. Even though I came of age in the 1970s and 1980s with the feminist movement and earned a degree in chemistry, I never developed a desire or ambition of my own. Too afraid to veer from what my mother and my church thought I "should" be, I never considered any other path than to be good, find a husband, and raise a family.

These "shoulds" led me to misbelieve that my worth was derived from being a wife and mother—certainly not from just being me. Just like Jim, my misbelief was so deep I didn't question it. To me, it was a fact in my life, a fact that would guide my behavior and decisions for decades.

In those years between our childhoods and our mid-forties, by all outward appearances and expectations, Jim and I were living the dream. He was a successful lawyer. I was a wife and mother at home with two children—a girl, Emma, and a boy, Dustin. It's just that we were living somebody else's dream for us—brought to reality by following our "shoulds" and perpetually powered by our respective fear loops. Though we didn't argue or blame each other, the tension, stress, and emotional distance inside our household and inside us was palpable—affecting us as a couple, as individuals, and most certainly affecting our children's wellbeing.

We've all in some way been touched by authoritarianism and the "shoulds." You may not have been physically punished with a belt or wooden spoon. You may have been given time-outs instead, which is progress to be sure. Still, the majority of us have been raised to conform and obey—in school, church, on the playground, if not at home. Most of us have experienced an authority figure's anger and shunning when we did something wrong, as well as praise and acceptance when we did something they liked, something they believed we "should" do. These emotional ways of control are authoritarian in their nature. Though not as outwardly severe as hitting, they still help you to form misbeliefs, coerce you into doing things because you "should," and inhibit your ability to develop a healthy and secure sense of self.

EVOLVING TOWARD SELF-RULE

Thankfully, as our society has become more child-centered, authoritarian parenting has given way to a more egalitarian approach—where each child is appreciated as an individual. We now have laws to protect children from abuse and neglect. Corporal punishment is frowned upon by society at large and officially by the American Psychological Association. (Though, as of this writing, around nineteen states still allow corporal punishment in schools.)

What science has uncovered about human development has likely played a big role here. We now accept that children are not born good or bad but are born having emotions—like fear, sadness, and joy. We have evidence that chronic stress leads to detrimental outcomes, both mentally and socially. We know that children thrive in safe environments.

Even our popular culture reflects this societal change. Disney Studios' 2021 release of *Encanto* is all about celebrating individuality and becoming who you are, not who you "should" be. Whereas twenty-five years earlier Scar was villainous in his rebellion against authority, *Encanto*'s heroine Mirabel saves her family, her entire community by questioning the status quo and standing up to her grandmother's authoritarianism. Through Mirabel's success, viewers get the message to trust in themselves.

If we are to evolve away from authoritarian rule and toward a more egalitarian and honest self-rule, we need to awaken the Mirabel inside of us. We need to question our status quo, rethink the "shoulds" in our lives, and make room for our authentic beliefs to emerge. Re-parenting is a way to get there.

BECOMING OUR OWN AUTHORITY—RE-PARENTING

My client Emily came to my practice because she wanted to start dating again after her recent divorce. She'd already downloaded a dating app and been out with a few guys. But she found going on dates was making her a nervous wreck. She reported that she worried incessantly about what her date thought of her, whether he liked her, and whether he thought she was pretty enough or interesting enough. Her nervousness and anxiety around this issue were evident as she talked. Both are expressions of fear, which is a clear sign of insecurity.

So in our first few sessions, I worked to bring Emily's focus back to herself, back to her own body. I asked her questions about her feelings, her needs, and her desires. As we combined this with some breathwork, she realized she hadn't thought about any of these things in a long, long time. She also realized that when it came to dating, her focus had been solely on her date's needs, not hers. "Why do I do that?" she asked me. "Why do I even care what some guy I don't really know thinks of me? And why does it upset me so much?"

To help Emily find answers to her questions, I taught her to re-parent herself. Over several sessions, I walked Emily through this process. I showed her how to go back and revisit herself as a child—to see things from that child's perspective, not her parents', and not her adult-self's.

Through re-parenting, Emily brought into her consciousness a misbelief she held all her life. From the time she was very young, she was taught that marriage was the only proper path for a girl and necessary for a girl's survival. She grew up misbelieving—as many girls do (including me)—that her only worth was as a married woman. So though now she was doing just fine as a single person, that misbelief—born of an authoritarian, patriarchal culture—was driving her behavior and desperation, preventing her from simply enjoying herself and her dates.

By exploring the fallacy of that misbelief over time, she gained a sense of self-worth from being herself. Her questions changed, as well. She started asking: "What kind of a man do I want to be with?" "What are some of my boundary rules for dating?" In time, an even bigger question came to her: "Do I even want to be married again?"

Today, Emily is dating. But she only dates men who she thinks highly of and finds attractive—not the other way around. She also makes time for friends and time for herself. Her goal is not to remarry because she "should" but to enjoy her life.

Through re-parenting, which she now knows how to do for herself, Emily feels worthy just the way she is. Nobody can judge her because she stopped judging herself. Re-parenting aided Emily in changing the focus of her attention—what psychologists call changing your "locus of control"—from the outside or extrinsic (what others wanted for her) to the inside of herself or intrinsic (what she decides she wants for herself).

When your locus of control is outside of your body, you feel insecure about everything. You worry what other people think of you. You are indecisive. You obsess over stupid mistakes. You're constantly under the stress of thinking you either don't belong or if people knew the real you, they would disapprove.

When your locus of control comes from inside yourself—which is what re-parenting develops—you look to yourself for answers and assessment. You ask questions such as: What am I feeling? What am I experiencing right now? How can I work through this problem? What do I want to do? Where do I want to go? What do I want to learn? What is best for me in this situation?

Somewhere inside you right now are your own memories, feelings, and perspective about what your childhood was like, what you were told, what you came to believe. When you take the time to explore that perspective, you, like Emily, find answers to the questions you have now, as well as new questions to ask. Re-parenting yourself is a natural process for that exploration. It's an inner journey of discovery to find the truth of who you are.

The trust you develop in yourself from knowing yourself then becomes the foundation of your self-worth, self-belonging, and self-assurance. As you leave the constraints of imposed authority behind and learn to follow your own inner guide, you find the guilt, the fear, and "shoulds" dissolve. You discover what you truly value and find the inner wisdom and strength to craft a life aligned with those values—a life that's yours.

TRY THIS: IDENTIFY YOUR "SHOULDS"
To get an idea where authoritarian rule might be preventing you from living fully, try this exercise:

- Step 1 – For the next forty-eight hours, become aware of every time you say, "I should."
- Step 2 – Write it down.
- Step 3 – After two days, take out your notes, ask these questions for each item, and write out your answers:

1. Why do I think I "should" do this?
2. How long have I thought this way?
3. Where does my insistence on doing this come from?
4. Do I want to do it?
5. Am I doing it to make myself happy? How will it make me happy?
6. Am I doing it to please someone else? To avoid judgment?
7. What would happen if I didn't do it? Is there fear involved in not doing it?
8. Could this "should" be a misbelief I hold? If so, what is the misbelief?

Keep these notes for reference as we work through the re-parenting process together.

3

YOUR INNER-CHILD

For most of my adult life, the mere mention of the term "inner-child" elicited an automatic eye roll from me. That's because for most of my adult life I was in a sect of Christianity that was suspicious of such psychological language. I'd spent decades training my mind to "think like Jesus" (which now seems irreverent, if not utterly sacrilegious). I'd look to the Bible to tell me what to think. When it came to the "inner-child," I took my cues from 1 Corinthians 13:11: "When I was a child, I spoke and thought and reasoned as a child. But when I grew up, I put away childish things." To me, "putting away childish things," meant shutting down (in other words, closing my mind to) any "psychobabble," "inner-child" nonsense.

But you don't have to be steeped in a religious belief system to consider the "inner-child" to be psychobabble. Lots of people view the term as a little woo. And it is the butt of more than a few jokes. That's because it's not only a funny sounding phrase, but it's ambiguous—which makes it easy to mock. People aren't clear on what the inner-child is and how it works within our individual psyche. Yet, the inner-child is the driver behind most of our thoughts, decisions, and behaviors.

MEETING MY INNER-CHILD

I met my inner-child for the first time at a seminar. As a newly minted psychotherapist—still in that Christian sect and mindset at the time—I went to a training on an emerging therapy based on Brainspotting. The technique uses our field of vision to unlock memories from the subcortical brain—the lower regions of the midbrain. Most things stored in the subcortical brain are not in our everyday awareness or consciousness. Through Brainspotting, clients can access those buried thoughts and feelings at their source almost instantly—as opposed to the months or even years talk therapy typically takes. The technique taught at the seminar I was attending that day didn't depend on the vision field alone to do this but used sensations from various areas of the body.

In the morning session, we watched a demonstration of the technique. A therapist called a volunteer from the audience on stage. After some deep breathing, the therapist had the volunteer inventory her body for any pain points and then focus on the one that was most pronounced. As the volunteer did that, she slowly began to curl up like a small, scared child. The therapist explained that the volunteer's attention to that area of her body had allowed her to tap into her inner-child and unlock buried emotions.

Inner-child, that's ridiculous, I thought. *That woman is making a fool of herself*. I wanted both the therapist and the volunteer to stop. I was so bothered (triggered) by what I'd witnessed that during the Q&A, I spoke up—something I never, ever did. And I was kind of obnoxious about it. I asked the psychologist whether she and the volunteer knew each other and if they'd planned the session. They assured me that what happened was spontaneous and very real. "Hmmm. Okay," I responded, with a slow nod of my head, but not really believing them or what I'd seen.

In the afternoon session, we attendees were to practice the technique on each other. As my practice partner and I sat knee to knee, we decided I'd play "the patient" first. I saw myself as nothing more than a prop for my partner to learn on—I certainly was not going to curl up in a ball of made-up emotions. My partner told me to close my eyes and take deep, slow breaths. I dutifully followed her instructions.

"Do you feel any pain in your body?" she asked.

Hmm, I thought. *How weird. I do feel pain.* "Yes," I replied. "My stomach feels tight."

"Okay, good." She then fiddled with her manual trying to find what to do next. After a long pause, she said, "Okay, now, keep feeling the tightness in your stomach and ask your body, 'How old do you feel?'"

Before I could ask myself that question, an image of me at six years old appeared in my head. I was lying in the dirt. I'd been grabbed and sexually assaulted by a teenage boy on my way home from school. Though I could see it all happening clearly, I had no words. All that came out of my mouth was, "I see me at six years old."

"Okay, good," my partner reassured me. Then, more waiting and rustling of papers. "Now," she said, "look into your six-year-old's eyes and breathe."

I followed her instructions all the while thinking this was a strange thing to do.

But when I looked into my six-year-old's eyes, my body shifted. I suddenly felt as if my fifty-year-old self was now inside my six-year-old's body. I felt the cold she felt. I felt the dirt. And then, oh, god, I felt her fear and shame. In my mind, tears streamed down my adult face. I couldn't stop them. I'd never cried over what happened to me before. At six, I hadn't had the knowledge or the words to understand the assault. All me-at-six felt was scared and alone—and now me-at-nearly-fifty knew that. As the tears flowed, it was as if a bubble I'd created forty-four years ago—a barrier six-year-old me had constructed between myself and the world—had burst. I did not hug my six-year-old self in my mind, and she did not run to me. We just stood there, an arm's distance apart, as I kept crying.

After a while, my practice partner's voice broke in, "Does your six-year-old want to tell her story? Maybe you can ask her."

Then, in my mind, Jesus (who at that time in my life would have represented my ultimate protector) appeared. He stood next to my six-year-old self and held her hand. She looked up at him and smiled. Adult me was still crying and unable to speak. But in my mind, I asked Jesus, "Were you there?" My face was a wet mess of tears and a runny nose, but I didn't care. It felt good somehow. I wasn't ashamed. I knew Jesus was there to help me.

"Yes," he said. "I was there with you."

That's all my six-year-old me needed to hear. That I hadn't been alone that day. It's what I'd needed to hear for decades. Knowing there had been the presence of another being when I was at my most scared and vulnerable calmed adult-me. My body relaxed and warmed up. I opened my eyes.

I don't know what my practice partner was doing that whole time. When I told her what happened, she was just as surprised as I was. I had not only met my inner-child at six years old, but I'd accessed her. Being able to understand the incident through her eyes and from her perspective, yet with my adult mind and experience, allowed me to start healing from a trauma that had been weighing me down and limiting me my whole life. This experience humbled me, to say the least.

WHO IS YOUR INNER-CHILD?

Your inner-child is not some abstract, new-age concept. It's not some excuse to elicit self-pity. And it's not psychobabble. It's simply memories of childhood experiences from your perspective at the age when they happened—not your current adult perspective. That's it.

When you are able tap into that, you put yourself on the most efficient route to bringing your negative misbeliefs into consciousness, where they can be examined. From there, you can re-parent that child you were, frame the incident properly, and free yourself to find the positive truth of who you are.

While the concept of the inner-child is simple, accessing that child's perspective isn't so obvious. Sometimes, we can recall the experiences themselves. But most of us cannot accurately recall the effects of an event on our younger selves—let alone the beliefs and strategies child-us (our inner-child) developed because of it. That takes some awareness and training.

For instance, as an adult, I was aware I'd been sexually assaulted as a small child. But I would have told anyone who asked that my assault had no effect on my present-day life. The story—given to me by my mother, my community, and fully adopted by me—was that the incident was behind me, and I was stronger for having survived. Adult-me was totally unaware that the beliefs adult-me lived by (you are alone in this world, the assault was all your fault, you are shameful) and coping strategies adult-me used all my life (be compliant; don't assert yourself; if you please others, they won't hurt you) were the creations of a scared six-year-old, left to find her own way in a dangerous world. Until I was open to meeting that six-year-old and seeing her truth—and mine—I'd be stuck living out those misbeliefs and strategies and going nowhere.

When you find yourself having disproportionally strong reactions to events or in a behavior pattern you can't shake, you're likely stuck in a belief system or coping strategy set by your inner-child long ago. One that made sense and worked for that child but no longer suits your reality.

My client Frank came to therapy because he was depressed about getting a divorce after thirty years of marriage. In our initial sessions, I learned that Frank had been raised in the Midwest in a churchgoing, farming community. He had a happy childhood, playing in wide-open spaces and working hard on the family farm. Hard work had high value for Frank. He believed—because it's what his parents, his church, his community preached—that if you live "right" and work hard, a good life will be yours. Up until now, his life had been a testament to that.

But here Frank was in the therapist's office, feeling worthless, lost, and depressed. He also felt confused. He just couldn't understand why his wife wanted a divorce. He had been a faithful husband and a good provider for every one of those thirty years. He'd done what he was supposed to do, and still she left and took her love with her.

After we'd worked together awhile, I invited Frank to try to find some insight into his situation through accessing his inner-child. He agreed. After some deep breathing, he met his ten-year-old self—who, like adult-Frank, felt lonely. Frank felt a tightness in his shoulders and neck. I told him to breathe into the tightness. He did and silently went on a journey with that ten-year-old. After a while, tears flowed down Frank's face.

When he opened his eyes, Frank told me that his ten-year-old had been standing in the rain. The child was cold and wet, holding a baseball glove. He was looking up as random people walked past him. His little self was hoping someone would stop for him, but everyone walked past. Then Frank saw his adult-self walking past the boy, pretending not to notice him. A thought came to adult-Frank: *This is not right*. Adult-Frank turned around, bent down, hugged his ten-year-old self, and took him home.

Then, Frank said to me, "It was me. It's been me all along."

"Yes, that's right. It's you that you needed all along," I replied.

Seeing himself through his ten-year-old's perspective, Frank realized that what that boy was really asking for was unconditional love—not love he had to earn by being dutiful. He saw that somewhere along the way that belief that "working hard was the path to the good life" got turned into the belief that love and connection had to be earned too. So when his wife left him, it's no wonder he felt worthless and lost.

But now he knew love can be unconditional. Moreover, he knew his adult-self had the ability to give that kind of love—and deserved to receive it. It wasn't a complete answer to Frank's issues, but it was a huge new awareness he could build on. Frank had re-parented his ten-year-old self and exposed a misbelief that was preventing him from understanding his current situation and healing. His inner-child helped Frank to change his view of love, and thus his view of divorce and himself. His inner-child showed Frank the way forward.

The younger you were when a belief planted itself in your brain, the further it probably is from your consciousness. But make no mistake, the memory of those instigating events and our child's perspective of them—the elements of our inner-child—are active in us today. Until we can call them into our consciousness and understand them (re-parent ourselves), we will continue to be ruled by what happened to us long ago.

HOW YOUR INNER-CHILD CAME TO BE

You have an inner-child for every moment of your childhood. They are with us from the second we come into the world (and maybe before)—taking in information, absorbing, and responding to the environment, looking for cause and effect, and devising ways to survive. Of course, the impression your inner-child takes away from an experience—and the beliefs and strategies they cultivate from it—depend on how developed their brain was at that time of the event. A ten-year-old inner-child is going to process an experience very differently than a six-year-old, who will draw different conclusions than an infant.

Human brains develop bottom-up and back to front—and won't be mature for twenty-six years on average. That's incredibly slow development as far as mammals go. For instance, puppies walk four weeks after birth. Elephant calves walk just two hours after birth. Comparatively, a human baby takes nine months to a year before having the neurological development to facilitate walking.

Our lower brain is working full tilt at birth, with our automatic nervous system controlling things like our breathing, heart rate, blood pressure, and digestion. But areas such as our mid-brain—with its subcortical structures like the limbic system that allow us to process short-term memories and emotions—take a little longer to get up to speed. While our neocortex and pre-frontal cortex—which control analytical thinking, calculating, reasoning, and decision-making—simply can't be depended on until young adulthood. So it should come as no surprise that, at any age, our inner-child doesn't have the brain function or the experiences needed to fully read a situation, weigh various aspects, and apply reason as an adult-you would before drawing conclusions.

Yet, it is in our childhood that the majority of our beliefs get established in our brains, long before we are capable of reason. Even more eye-opening, it is in those first three years of life—with our limited vocabulary and even more limited experience—that most of our neural connections form. And because the more a connection gets used the stronger it becomes, those early connections become foundational for the beliefs and strategies that follow. In other words, much of what is driving you to think as you do and make the choices you make today is coming from an infant's perspective—or toddler's perspective at best. Which, if you think about it, explains a lot about the human condition. (We'll explore how the parent/baby relationship informs these foundational beliefs in the next chapter.)

As you move toward re-parenting, you always want to stay alert to the age of the inner-child you're encountering and consider how a child of that age thinks, so you see things from their perspective. That inner-child holds your uncorrupted memories. They hold your uncorrupted experience. They hold your uncorrupted thoughts and conclusions that made perfect sense to them in their time. When you can look at it all from their perspective, they also hold answers you need to free yourself from any misbeliefs or patterns planted long ago.

RECONNECTING TO YOUR INNER-CHILD

Through your inner-child, you have the opportunity to take another look at what happened to you, to see the truth, to make a different neural connection, and heal the pain. But most of us don't know to go there, and anyway, we've lost touch with who we were. Sometimes because the memories are too painful. Sometimes because those experiences are such a part of who we are that we can't imagine another way.

Whether or not we acknowledge an inner-child, make no mistake we are in a relationship with them. Though I denied my inner-child's existence, I still lived by the belief system that child had given me—a belief system that kept me a child of sorts, dependent on others, ashamed of myself, thinking I couldn't take care of myself.

I don't recommend reconnecting with your inner-child abruptly, unexpectedly, and, at first, through a traumatic event like I did. But I do recommend both acknowledging your inner-child and getting to know them. Start gently with simple awareness. Awareness that your inner-child exists. Awareness that the beliefs and strategies that helped you when you were young might need to be reassessed. Your inner-child is with you right now, waiting for you to take their pain, so they can relieve yours.

TRY THIS: REMEMBERING YOURSELF

This exercise is a warmup for meeting your inner-child(ren). It should help you remember what it was like to be you as a child at every stage of development.

- Step 1 – Gather early childhood photos of yourself from birth through high school.

    Put them in chronological order.

- Step 2 – Pick up each photo, one at a time.

    Look at that child's face.

- Step 3 – For each age (including high school), note how innocent, helpless, and dependent you were.

    Think about what you knew of the world then and what you didn't. Make a note to remember that as you move into re-parenting yourself.

- Step 4 – Remember who you were when the photo was taken.

    Look at your clothing and surroundings in each photo. What was your life like? What brought you joy? What worried you?

What talents did you have? What talents did you use? What were you scared of? What were you interested in? What pressures did you have? What were your hopes for the future?

4

RE-PARENTING YOURSELF

Your inner-child was parented by your parents or guardians. If you've never been in touch with your inner-child, chances are that child is still believing, behaving, and reacting according to your parents' or guardians' wishes for you, not yours.

I believe most parents love their children, want the best for them, and do the best they can by them. I also believe that as parents, we don't always know what's best. How can we? Parents are only human. We get a lot wrong. I know how much I love my own children. I also know that when I look back on parenting them, there are some behaviors I had and decisions I made that I'd change if I could. If you're a parent, I'm sure that's true for you, too.

As in all human interactions, your parents brought their whole selves to their relationship with you. Their ideas about how to be a good parent, their hopes for you, their expectations for you were products of how they'd been parented themselves, as well as their experiences growing up and in their adult lives. For some, that may have included things like trauma, their own stressful family relationships, cultural expectations, and poor social support.

We do ourselves and our parents a disservice when we refuse to see them as human. We leave no room for real connection when we insist our childhoods were without fault and our parents perfect. I put my own parents on a pedestal for the first forty-eight years of my life. I would not allow anyone—but most especially myself—to question their parenting. Which meant I didn't question myself or my beliefs about the world. I thought I was protecting my parents. But all I was really protecting was some idealized version of them that negated the reality of the trauma both had suffered in life. This self-serving fantasy—which my parents encouraged through their own stories and behaviors—allowed me to prop up my misbelief that all was well in our household and that I was "good."

If we don't examine the past (what happened to us), we never see the truth of it. So we can't come to understand it on our own terms. We don't heal and move forward from it. Also, when we refuse or aren't allowed to see our parents as people, there's no chance for true intimacy, understanding, or connection with them.

Re-parenting yourself is not about calling out what your parents did wrong or blaming them. No parent can prepare a child for every possibility in life or know how a child might perceive an event. Your parents couldn't know what your childhood looked like from your perspective—what events affected you (maybe even traumatized you), which made you feel secure, which have stayed with you into adulthood, or what you choose to believe based on your experiences.

For those who were sexually abused, physically abused, or emotionally abused by your parents, re-parenting isn't about reaching forgiveness. It's about freeing yourself from past circumstances. It's about understanding that how you were parented likely did not start with your childhood but was the result of trauma passed down from generation to generation. With that insight, not only can you heal and reclaim your life, but you can make sure your generation is the last in your family to be harmed by such transgenerational traumas.

Healing requires we take an honest look at our childhood—including the mistakes our parents made and any misinterpretations we made. Through re-parenting, we can step out of our fear loop, come to understand the reality of what happened to us, and bring our belief system into alignment with who we authentically are.

THE RE-PARENTING MODEL

Re-parenting is a reverse engineering process that combines what we know about human development and neurobiology to change misbeliefs and patterned behaviors that no longer serve us into beliefs and strategies that do. It doesn't simply focus on the past. It uses that past to shine a light on why you currently frame the world the way you do. It lets you explore how you might want to adjust that frame to more accurately reflect you and the world you live in.

When you re-parent yourself, you replace the original relationship you had as a child with your parent with a new relationship between your adult-self and your child-self or inner-child. Your adult-self—your bigger, stronger, wiser self—becomes the parent your inner-child can now turn to for security and guidance. Re-parenting won't change all your childhood beliefs and strategies, just the ones that push you into your fear loop and keep you there. Psychologists call this kind of process a "corrective emotional experience."

The re-parenting method I use in my practice—and what you'll learn in upcoming chapters—grew organically from what I learned on my own healing journey and now use with my clients. The process merges several evidence-based, mind-body therapies with well-established parenting and child-development theories.

MEETING THE MOMENT

For most of my life, I froze at the mention of the sexual assault I'd experienced as a child. That's because trauma forces our attention outside the body—causing us to dissociate our mind. In a protective action to keep us from reliving the traumatic incident, our nervous system dysregulates into fight, flight, freeze, or faint (FFFF response). Whenever my body froze, my mind would reel with the thoughts I'd formed the day the assault happened—fear, shame, self-hatred. Automatically,

I'd take immediate action to keep myself safe, whether or not that's what the situation called for. In my case, this meant becoming as invisible as possible. Well into my adulthood (before I entered therapy), that freeze response was still protecting me. It was also keeping me from living my life.

Mind-body therapies begin with stopping us from dissociating (not getting lost in our fear loop or our FFFF response). They bring our attention back to our body, so our mind and body can stay connected. Using a physical prompt, they enable us to resource, regulate, and calm our nervous system. As we leave our fear loop and come fully (mentally and physically) into the present moment, adult-us gets the opportunity to locate our inner-child, examine our inner-child's feelings, and work toward releasing them. The mind-body therapies I use in my practice—individually and in combination, depending on a client's needs—include:

- Eye Movement Desensitization and Reprocessing (EMDR), which works through bilateral eye movement while recounting a traumatic event.
- Brainspotting, which is similar to EMDR but uses several static eye positions to release the trauma.
- Emotional Freedom Technique—also known as "tapping"—which uses sequenced tapping of fingers on a surface.
- And breathing techniques.

Mind-body therapies are more efficient than talk therapies because they're more direct. Often what happened to us in the past is hard to put into words. Some experiences are no longer in our conscious memory. Some were so traumatic or emotional that words aren't sufficient. Further, if a significant event happened when we were very young, we might not have had the vocabulary or the life experience to know what really happened, let alone create and store an accurate memory of it.

But the feelings an event produced—joy, fear, love, anger—remain.

The negative emotions often manifest themselves in later life as a physical pain or constriction in the body. Thus, our body becomes the most efficient route to bringing the truth of what happened into our consciousness where it can be processed.

WHERE DOES IT HURT?

Carrie came to my practice because she was in a verbally and psychologically abusive relationship. She wanted to end it but felt so scared of her boyfriend's reaction if she broke up with him that she froze at the thought of confronting him. In our first several sessions, Carrie learned to use both breathing exercises and EMDR to regulate her reaction, get out of her fear loop, unfreeze, and reconnect her mind and body.

In a subsequent session, after she employed those mind-body therapies and self-regulated, I asked Carrie to imagine telling her boyfriend that she wanted him to move out. As she did that, I asked where she "felt" that request in her body. "I feel tightness in my throat, jaw, and neck," she reported. I then encouraged Carrie to focus her attention on that tightness.

In doing so, an incident when she was eleven years old came into her mind. She'd been grounded but had snuck out her window into her yard to talk with some friends. As she was laughing with them, she suddenly felt her hair being grabbed from behind. It was her father. He yanked her head back violently. As he dragged her into the house by her hair, Carrie felt a sharp pain in her neck, along with his anger. She was afraid of what he would do because she'd disobeyed him. She knew from experience that whenever she challenged his authority, his go-to response was typically physical and violent.

As Carrie began to cry at these memories, I encouraged her to stay in her body and breathe through the pain. Using a breathing exercise, she once again regulated herself. From there, with her focus back on the pain in her jaw and neck, she was able to connect to her inner-eleven-year-old and re-parent the misbelief that she would be physically hurt if she didn't go along with what others wanted.

In time, Carrie came to understand the connection her brain was making between her fear of her father and her fear of her boyfriend. She could see how the experiences she'd had all those years ago were keeping her compliant as an adult. With this knowledge, Carrie was able to heal her inner-child and replace her misbelief with the truth—that she deserved to be loved and treated with respect in relationships, and that all men were not her father. Over time with this new understanding, Carrie gained the self-love and resolve to tell her boyfriend the relationship was over and he needed to move out.

But Carrie's re-parenting work didn't end there—and yours won't end with one breakthrough at one point in childhood either. Her eleven-year-old self and the tightness in her throat were merely her first access points to myriad misbeliefs and obsolete strategies that were causing her adult-self trouble in life and keeping her stuck. Her relationship with her father didn't start when she was eleven and so neither did the belief system she constructed from that relationship.

GETTING TO THE CORE

No matter what age our inner-child is when we first access them, to fully heal a misbelief or obsolete strategy, we must return to where it began, its foundation. Which means re-parenting thought patterns created in infancy—when our first neural connections were established.

When we are infants, our parents generate almost all our experiences. Thus, it's mostly their actions that determine which of our neural connections get made and strengthened in those first critical years. So the quality of our bond with our parents—whether or not we can depend on them—becomes the foundation of our later behaviors and worldview. These early childhood interactions form what psychologists call our "attachment style"—attachment being the invisible string, the emotional connection between us and our parents or caregivers.

Imagine baby-you experiencing pain. You squiggle around, tense up, and begin to cry. You hear your mom's voice. "What's the matter, sweety?" You sense her nearby and turn your head, your eyes searching for her. She bends over you and touches your head softly. "Do you need your diaper changed?" she asks. Your body relaxes as she touches and speaks to you. You feel a little better, but the pain is still there so you cry again. Mom picks you up and bounces you on her shoulder. You feel the pain get worse and cry louder. "What's the matter?" Mom says. She turns you over on her lap, pats you softly on your back. Suddenly, gas escapes out of your mouth and the pain disappears. "Great burp! Good job!" she says, as she brings your face close to hers and smiles. You look at her and smile back. You feel happy and warm. She holds you, kisses you, then lays you back down with a toy. You reach for the toy.

Though you have no language, baby-you still forms beliefs about yourself and the world from this interaction. If your mother is consistent in her attention (she doesn't need to be perfect here, just consistent), she makes you feel safe in the world. As you take in information on how to survive, your direct experience makes neural connections to inform which actions and decisions are called for. From these experiences, baby-you lays down some strategies for the future: I will cry when I am in pain. I can trust Mom to come and relieve my pain. I am worthy of paying attention to. The world is a safe place where my needs will be met.

Now imagine if your parents aren't consistent with their care or are neglectful with you—for whatever reason (illness, having to work, other children needing care, ignorance of how to care for a baby, etc.). What if no one came when you cried, when you were hungry, or when you had a soiled diaper? What if you couldn't be sure that relief was on its way? What if your parent always came and attended to you, but never cuddled you or talked to you or looked at you really because their own mind is overwhelmed and burdened with worries about money or domestic abuse or the demands of parenting other children? If that were the case, baby-you would come to very different conclusions about how the world works, the tactics needed for survival, and your own self-worth.

Using the conclusions babies draw from interactions with their parents and the lifelong behaviors that manifest from them, psychologists have identified four styles or patterns of "attachment."

- Secure attachment—This pattern is created when an infant is cared for by an attentive parent who is reliable and emotionally available. These children learn they can trust in other people and the world. Securely attached babies tend to grow into adults with the self-love and confidence needed to engage in healthy relationships, as well as navigate disappointment and tragedy.
- Insecure-anxious attachment—This anxious pattern results when parents are inconsistent with care or conditional with their love. These children blame themselves for their parents' neglect. They work to win back their parents' love and attention—which results in self-esteem issues and fear of abandonment. As adults, they need a great deal of reassurance in relationships. When negative things happen, they head to self-blame, where they don't find a healthy solution or resilience.
- Insecure-avoidant attachment—This pattern occurs when the primary caregiver is emotionally unavailable. These children resort to suppressing their feelings. They idealize their parents and their childhoods. They often describe their upbringing in vague terms like "great" and "can't complain." They grow into highly independent adults with big trust issues. They're conflicted in that they feel intense loneliness but are never fully able to invest themselves in relationships.
- Disorganized attachment—This pattern results from extreme trauma, abuse, and/or abandonment by parents or a primary caregiver—disrupting and harming the child's natural drive to connect to their parent. For these children, relationships become triggers causing them to dissociate. They can become

anti-social. Some fail to develop empathy and grow up to be abusers themselves.

Attachment styles show us that no person is born bad or rebellious. Rather we are all born with needs. How we behave is the product of our experience in getting those needs met. Our attachment style is set through a process called synaptic pruning. Just like a tree's dead limbs are cut back or pruned to promote a stronger tree, our baby brain prunes away the connections we don't use much in favor of those we do.

If we've never interrupted those "favored" synapses, then as adults our attachment style is still driving our behavior. By understanding our attachment style, we can better understand why certain events send us into our fear loop or why we have trouble with relationships. As we work to re-parent ourselves, it's helpful to see ourselves through the lens of our attachment style at different ages and through various challenges.

For example, Carrie likely experienced her father's explosive anger from infancy on. From his outburst, baby-Carrie learned she could not be sure of a person's reactions (especially a man's) and so developed an insecure-attachment pattern. Those neural connections—which developed in her a sensitivity to a loud male voice—then informed her reactions to her father when she was eleven. In adulthood, this subconscious pattern also left her open to abusive relationships—because to her, abuse was "normal." In addition, this attachment style made her cautious, disempowered, and vulnerable when it came to making her needs known, as evidenced by her fear of confronting her boyfriend. If Carrie never did the work to go beyond her inner-eleven-year-old to re-parent her inner-infant and form truer, more useful beliefs, that patterned thinking would've continued popping up and inhibiting her for the rest of her life.

Luckily for Carrie—and all of us—we can re-parent our attachment style and build a new network of synapses that better fit our adult lives.

TAKING ON THE PARENTAL ROLE

Just like the relationship between you and your parents grew day by day, your new re-parented relationship with yourself will grow interaction by interaction. With each parental contact with your inner-child, your mind and body will be better able to let go of misbeliefs about who you thought you were or thought you should be, so you can be more fully who you are.

All human beings need attentive, loving, responsive care to grow into mature, realized adults. Wherever you didn't have that as an infant or child, re-parenting allows you to give that to yourself now. Your journey to get there will be unique to you and the factors of your life. Your body—where you feel tightness and pain—will guide you to what needs your attention.

No matter how much you love your family or how hard your parents tried, every childhood has some kind of trauma, unresolved pain, and misunderstandings. As you heal these experiences one by one through re-parenting, you will develop resilience, self-confidence, and a better relationship with yourself and the world. You will stop reacting without thinking and start having agency in your own life.

The re-parenting process is not a miracle cure. It is not some mystical, magical, out-of-body experience. How you were parented informs every cell in your body. So re-parenting demands your willingness to look at and connect with every part of yourself at every age (infant, toddler, small child, grade-school child, pre-teen, adolescent), conscious and subconscious, body and mind. Like any productive therapy, re-parenting takes time, effort, and commitment on your part. After all, you're taking on the responsibility to re-raise yourself.

Once you learn the re-parenting process, however, you can use it for any situation, any pain, any difficulty for the rest of your life. With each nurturing interaction between you and your inner-child, you strengthen the neural pathways in your brain that are most advantageous to your life now. Your healing will build upon itself, creating momentum with every interaction as you step away from old, unhelpful thought patterns to become more fully who you are.

TRY THIS: SELF-REGULATING WITH BREATHING TECHNIQUES

Whether you're aware of it or not, you probably already use breathing to regulate your nervous system—taking a breath and counting to ten when you are angry, letting out a big sigh when you are frustrated, or breathing into a paper bag when you are emotionally overwhelmed. When we control our breath, we integrate all three parts of our brain—the brain stem, midbrain, and our neocortex—to achieve self-regulation.

The four breathing techniques below—Heart Breathing, Ocean Breathing, Earth Breathing, Fire Breathing—all offer a way to become even more intentional and efficient in using your breath to bring your brain and body back to center.

Try them all. Note how each makes you feel. Use as needed to self-regulate.

- Heart Breathing—This is the breath I use most often with clients and with myself. It's a nurturing breath. You start by sitting in a chair with your feet on the floor. Breathe naturally and become present in your body. When you're ready, take in a breath through your nose from the air above your head and below your feet. Place this breath in your heart and hold for a count of four. Exhale through your mouth, while picturing the breath flowing from your heart—out the front of your body and the back. Send that breath—your breath—wherever it needs to go in your body. Repeat until you feel calm and cared for.
- Ocean Breathing—A breath for soothing and releasing stress, this breath mimics the rhythm of ocean waves, as its name suggests. To do it, sit in a comfortable chair. Close your eyes. Settle into your body. Slow your natural breath. Feel your diaphragm

move as you breathe. Now, as you think of the movement of the ocean, breathe in through your nose for a count of five. Feel your diaphragm rise as you take in air. As you exhale out of your mouth, restrict the back of the throat so your exhalation makes a little noise—like a wave hitting the shore. Feel your diaphragm lower as you breathe out to a count of six. Focus on this rhythm. Think about the movement of the ocean. Continue doing this until you feel calm and centered.

- Earth Breathing—Use this grounding breath when you feel unbalanced, anxious, or flighty. Start by sitting in a comfortable chair with both feet on the floor. Close your eyes and get in touch with your breath and your body. Choose one foot to receive the earth's energy on your inhale and the other foot to release any negative energy on the exhale. As you breathe in, feel the energy of the earth coming up through your foot. Let it move through your leg to your spine—and hold it there. After four counts, release the breath, let it move down the other leg and out the other foot to return to the earth. Repeat until you feel grounded.
- Fire Breathing—Because this breath brings about release and clarity, it's commonly used in therapy. Whenever you feel muddled or burdened, you can use fire breath to get you back into an open state of mind. Begin as always by sitting comfortably and getting in touch with your natural breath and body. When you are ready, inhale through the nose. As you take air in, fill your belly full of it. Once full, exhale quickly from the back of the throat, deflating your belly and pulling it in toward the spine. Unlike the other breathing techniques, Fire Breathing is forceful and explosive. You should feel the chaotic energy leaving your body.

5

RE-PARENTING YOUR INNER-INFANT (AGES 0-1)

As a young mother, I really did not understand how much my babies needed me. I'm a little embarrassed to admit this, but I didn't think babies could or would remember anything. I didn't think what happened to them in those first years was all that important. I couldn't recall anything about when I was a baby, so I figured my children wouldn't either. (I never was curious enough to investigate my early childhood experiences either.)

Of course, I was completely wrong. Thankfully, most parents and people today know our experiences in the first few years of life are foundational to us as human beings. The science demonstrating this keeps growing. The fact is we do remember what happens to us when we are infants and toddlers. It's just that the way we store and recall those infant memories is different than what we typically think of as memory.

Human beings have two types of memories—autobiographical and procedural, or subconscious memories. Autobiographical memories are what most of us think of when we think of memory. They're created and stored in the top part of the brain (our neocortex) and are brought into our consciousness using language—making them easy to access and process. We usually recall, re-experience, and retell these memories in story form. We don't create autobiographical memories in our infancy because our neocortex is still under construction and we don't yet have language.

Procedural or subconscious memories form in our brain stem and our limbic or mid-brain—the reactive and emotional parts of the brain, the parts infants use most. Procedural memories result from events we can't (or our brain doesn't want to) put into words—such as traumatic events and things that happen before we have words. These memories are stored in our bodies. When something stirs them and causes them to resurface, they resurface as feelings. If the memory is of a negative, scary, or confusing event, it might manifest as a tightening in the throat or chest, hair standing up on the back of your neck, a sudden queasiness in the stomach, or an overall feeling of anxiety. Though most people experience these sensations from time to time, they go through life unaware such memories are there, let alone that those memories continue to determine their decisions and actions.

As we've discussed, the process of re-parenting makes the unconscious conscious, so we can know what we think, take a look at it, and reframe through our adult lens any thoughts or beliefs that no longer serve us. You, of course, re-parent yourself at whatever age calls to you. But because these infant memories are foundational, recalling and then re-parenting them is an opportunity to correct misbeliefs that have followed you through every stage of development, keeping you stuck in your fear loop. The sooner in the re-parenting process you can get to your inner-infant, the more productive and efficient the entire re-parenting process will be for you.

HOW YOUR FOUNDATIONS FORM

As human beings, our brain's primary task is our physical survival. Instinctively, in any situation, the first question your brain asks is: "Am I safe?" If you are, your brain then moves to the next question in the hierarchy of survival: "Am I loved?" Being loved and belonging furthers our chances of making it in this world. Only when those two survival needs are satisfied, do we go to the last question: "Can I learn?" If we are to survive as we mature and become independent of our caregivers, we need to learn about the world we're part of and how to take care of ourselves in it. These questions are unconscious and instinctual, and our brain asks them throughout our lives from the moment we are born.

When you live inside your mother's womb, all your body's needs are taken care of. You are safe. You do belong—your body literally being part of your mom's body. Her body makes sure that your body is regulated—meaning it's not in distress and has all it needs to survive and thrive. The womb protects you from the demands and assaults of the world.

Once outside the womb, however, your body experiences all kinds of sensations—including unpleasant ones such as cold, pain, hunger, scary sounds, glaring lights, and wet diapers. At the same time, your body's systems (digestive, nervous, cardio, pulmonary, immune, etc.) become activated and need things from the world to function and keep you alive. When infant-you has a need—say you are hungry or cold—you become distressed and your system becomes dysregulated. You are not safe. So your nervous system sends out the alarm to fix whatever is wrong.

But infant-you does not yet have the ability to meet your own needs, regulate your body, or get back to a neutral set point for your body by yourself. You need a parent or caregiver for that. So you cry out for one. If you have a parent or caregiver that responds to your cry and meets your physical needs with consistency, infant-you feels safe. With additional helpings of hugs, tenderness, and joy from your caregiver, you also feel loved. Your nervous system deactivates, and your body regulates. You are calm. With each round of "cry out, help come, problem solved, and kisses," you become less anxious and develop the secure attachment we talked about in the previous chapter. With that, you now have the energy to learn.

Because these thought processes are the first neural connections you form in your brain, they become foundational to how you think as you grow. The more secure and less stressed infant-you was, the more secure and less stressed toddler-you, child-you, and adult-you likely were and are. These foundational impressions made in infancy set the tone for your life.

The importance of the parent-infant relationship in keeping infants feeling secure and so regulated is illustrated by developmental psychologist Edward Tronic's famous Still Face Experiment. In the first part of the experiment, moms look into their baby's eyes and reflect the baby's expression or respond to their child's motions. For instance, if the baby smiles, the mom smiles back. If the baby coos, the mom coos back. If the baby points, the mom looks to where the baby points. In videos of these experiments, you can see the baby's nervous system is calm. The baby is happy and engaged during this first phase.

In the second part of the experiment, the mom looks into her baby's eyes but keeps her face still with a neutral expression and does not reflect the baby's expression back. Within moments, the baby becomes distressed. Their nervous system is activated. As they become more dysregulated, they cry out. As soon as the mom breaks her still face and responds to the baby with concern and a loving touch, the baby calms down and is regulated again. (You can view a host of videos of this experiment for yourself on YouTube.)

But imagine if this weren't an experiment. Imagine this is real life with a mom who is suffering with her own trauma, post-partum depression, or is just ignorant that her baby needs her emotional attention. Imagine a mom who cannot or does not respond to the baby. The baby would be left in distress. After this happens several times, the baby would conclude that when they cry out, no one comes, and so the world is not safe and they are not loved. Those would be the first neural connections formed in that baby's brain. Fear would become foundational to how that baby approached the world as they grew. Insecurity would set the tone for their life, causing all kinds of troubles.

REGULATION, NOT CONTROL

Of course, we don't spend our lives depending on our parents to keep us warm, fed, and dry. However, what we experience when they are in charge of regulating our systems does affect how we approach our own self-regulation as we grow. We learn to self-regulate by first co-regulating with our parents or caregiver. They model for us how to care for ourselves and even what to think about ourselves.

Where many parents go wrong in our culture is in not understanding the difference between encouraging self-control and encouraging self-regulation in meeting their children's needs. Control is imposed from the outside, even when it's self-control. Regulation—the true aim for optimal survival—is an internal motivation.

When a parent complains to me that their child is "out of control," my first thought is that the child is not out of control, they are dysregulated. Nobody wants to act out, throw a tantrum, or be self-destructive; none of those things feel good. Those are all signs that a child, a teenager, or an adult is frustrated and can't regulate themselves back to a neutral set point. Most likely, that's because they were raised on self-control to manage their emotions and reactions, instead of learning to self-regulate.

For instance, when we were new parents, Jim and I worried a lot about "spoiling" our children. (We bought into the fallacy that you can spoil a baby. You can't.) At the time, we were big into our church and wanted to be good Christian parents. We wanted our babies to meet our ideal of good behavior, so they'd be accepted in society and live good lives. We placed a high value on obedience as a way to achieve that.

First on our agenda was getting our children on a sleep schedule. With both births, days after bringing them home from the hospital, we began sleep "training" our babies, believing with all our hearts we were doing what was best for each of them. When we put these brand-new beings to bed for the night, we closed the door, and let them cry it out. Yes, it was hard on us to hear them cry. But the Christian parenting books we were reading assured us we were teaching them to self-soothe, which would be important in their becoming self-reliant. Our underlying fear—one we shared with many parents at that time—was that if we didn't establish these habits in infancy, our children would be undisciplined and unable to take care of themselves.

Today, Jim and I both understand that that's not how this works. In fact, it's the opposite. When we are born, our brains are all instinct and instant response (the limbic and mid-brain). Remember, the neocortex (which we need for reasoning and self-control) isn't even functional yet. So think about what that sleep "training" felt like from our babies' perspective. When Jim or I laid them down to sleep, we patted their backs, kissed their heads, and said good night. Then we left them alone. As adults with reason and experience, we knew our babies were safe and that we were nearby if they were in danger. But our infants didn't know that. All they knew is that they were left alone and helpless in a dark room. So they felt alone and helpless. They learned that when they cry, no one is coming. Eventually, they fell asleep—but it wasn't from self-soothing, it was from exhaustion from crying. Worse, they likely never slept deeply because their nervous systems were still activated, not regulated. Instead of learning to self-soothe, they learned to sleep with one eye open. Inadvertently, Jim and I created an insecure foundation in both our children. "Slightly on edge" became their baseline of safety.

Responding to a baby's needs is how you help them become secure in the world. With that foundation to stand on, they can become confident, resilient children and adults who trust themselves and know they can look to themselves for direction. Trying to control their behavior from infancy is how you lay the foundation for an adult who is always looking outside themselves—looking for rules or authority figures—to tell them how to behave. Such an adult is susceptible to influences, both good and bad.

As we've discussed, my parents raised me to obey—and I did. But for decades of my life, my obeying was merely a reaction to the threat of rejection. Throughout my childhood and the majority of my adult life, I never did things because that's what I felt my body needed or that's what I wanted for my life. My identity was not my own but merely a reflection of their expectations. Because I was habituated to look outside myself to regulate my life, I employed my self-control to push away any thoughts that didn't conform to the rules others set for me. The result was a person out of alignment with her true nature. I was always looking over my shoulder, worried if I was "doing life right," and looking for confirmation that I was. My nervous system was always on alert looking for the next threat and working overtime to hide the real me from this world and from myself.

This is the damage done by promoting self-control from infancy. Our brains don't develop the neural pathways for self-regulation. Infants whose parents worked to control their behaviors become children and then adults who wait to react to whatever happens to them. They don't feel they have agency in their life to act on what they desire. Without internal motivation and the ability to self-regulate, so much in life becomes a struggle. Willpower is only so powerful.

My story is not an uncommon one. You may even recognize yourself in it. Until I got into therapy and re-parented my inner-infant away from self-control and toward self-regulation, I had no idea how to accept my thoughts—all of them—to trust them and integrate them into my identity and my life. When we learn to listen to ourselves, to believe in ourselves, and respond to our needs, we come to know who we are and what is right for us.

RE-PARENTING YOUR INNER-INFANT

However, getting in touch with our inner-infant—let alone re-parenting that part of ourselves—can be challenging. Since we don't have autobiographical memories of that time in our lives, we have to pay extra attention to our physical feelings for what our inner-infant needs from adult-us.

In infancy, you were learning to focus your sight, recognize sounds, identify smells, use your taste, and feel the world around you. Your digestive system was learning to intake food, absorb nutrients, and expel waste. Internally, your nervous system was trying to establish a comfortable rhythm for all this eating, digesting, expelling, and sleeping, as well as find dependable patterns in your caregiver's behaviors. So much of our early development is about finding balance, physically and emotionally.

Thus in our adult life, when we find ourselves out of balance, that's a clue that an idea or misbelief formed in our infancy could be directing a behavior or creating a pattern in our life that's causing issues for us today. If you find yourself having digestion problems (eating too much or too little, nausea), breathing difficulties (trouble catching your breath or asthma), sensitivity to your environment (bothered by touch, sounds, lights, or smells), or are unusually clumsy (having repetitive accidents, falls, or injuries), you might want to get in touch with your inner-infant. All of these are physical functions that developed alongside our first neural pathways.

My client Judy shared in therapy that she'd had a series of car accidents lately, in which she repeatedly hurt her left knee. As she told me about these accidents, she also remembered that she'd hurt that same knee in high school playing tennis. So I had her focus on her knee and ask herself how old she felt. Her response surprised us both. She said she felt like a baby. With that revelation, the pain spread from her knee to her hip, and she felt the need to kick, which I encouraged her to do.

As she kicked, we practiced some fire-breathing exercises—the fast-paced breathing that releases extra energy and brings balance to the sympathetic and parasympathetic nervous systems. I then had her imagine cuddling and holding her infant-self. She reported infant-her felt angry. So we did more Fire Breathing, until we calmed (regulated) her inner-infant.

After the session, she told me infant-her was angry at her dad though she didn't know why. I suggested she write a letter to her father expressing that anger. (The letter was for therapeutic reasons only. She was not to mail it.) To this day, she doesn't know what happened between infant-her and her father to cause such anger. But by recognizing a pattern of injury, regulating her inner-infant, and allowing herself to feel what she felt back then, she was able to release and heal repressed anger from infancy, regulate her adult-self, and move forward in her life from a more balanced place.

ATTUNING TO YOUR INNER-INFANT. BUILDING A BOND WITH YOURSELF.

For Judy—and all of us—the transformation we seek for our lives doesn't come from changing an outward behavior or following a new set of rules. Anyone who has ever dieted, tried to break a habit, or suffered with an addiction can tell you that. We must change ourselves on the inside to achieve and sustain the outcomes we want.

To re-parent our inner-infant, we, too, must turn inward. When we can re-examine our infancy and come to terms with the circumstances that formed our foundational misbeliefs, we are able to reinterpret and heal foundational wounds.

Just like any parent of a newborn, your job here is to do for your inner-infant what they can't do for themselves. You must acknowledge their pain, figure out and eliminate its source, regulate them, and rebuild their current attachment style into a secure one.

Denise came to therapy to get over the depression that resulted from breaking up with her boyfriend, who was emotionally abusive toward her. She was in a cycle of behavior she described to me as self-destructive. She was going to bars, having a few drinks, and finding different guys to take her home. She was self-aware enough to know this behavior was a reaction to her fear of being alone. She also knew she'd never find the lasting relationship she craved through these hook-ups.

Denise had tried using self-control. She'd promised herself she'd stop going home with men she didn't know or care about. But then she'd find herself in a bar—swearing to herself that she was just there for a drink and some company. And the next thing she knew, she'd be waking up in a stranger's bed. Her lack of "willpower" (her words, not mine) made her feel lonelier and full of self-contempt.

Denise was trying to "control" herself. Even if she had kept her promise to herself not to go out—she'd still have been left at home feeling lonely and without connection. Self-control would not solve her underlying distress, her inability to sustain a healthy relationship, and ultimately her fear of abandonment—a fear that hinted she'd developed an insecure-attachment style as an infant. If she were going to achieve the outcomes she desired for her life, she'd have to change from the inside.

Denise knew that as a child she'd felt both unwanted and unloved. She'd tried hard throughout her life to not think about that. Intellectually, adult-Denise understood that her mother had suffered from (and still did) severe depression and wasn't to blame for being emotionally unavailable to Denise throughout her childhood. But it's likely that Denise's inner-child—most especially her inner-infant—did not share this same understanding.

Using breathwork to help her attune to physical sensations in her body, Denise began the process of re-parenting her inner-child. Her five-year-old self was the first to come to her. That five-year-old believed (or misbelieved) that her mom liked her younger sister better because her sister was better than she was. That's the way five-year-old Denise made sense of the mother's emotional distance. Adult-Denise was able to assure her five-year-old self that nothing could be further from the truth. She was able to help her inner-child shift that belief and realize that her mother's inattentiveness was due to mental-health issues and had nothing to do with Denise or her sister.

But it wasn't until Denise experienced the fear her inner-infant had felt that she understood what was driving her current-day behavior. No matter how hard infant-Denise cried, she could not count on anyone responding to her needs. When her mother finally did show up with a bottle or a clean diaper, there were no hugs, no cooing, nothing to make infant-Denise feel safe and loved. Instead, she felt like a burden.

Being able to re-parent that sense of abandonment, to regulate her infant-self (and thus her adult-self), and to acknowledge that foundational fear was the start of Denise changing her life for the better. Denise learned to delight in and welcome her inner-infant. In her mind, Denise would put her inner-infant in her arms, cuddle her, and naturally synch their breathing and heart rates. She'd look into the infant's eyes and tell her inner-infant things her mother wasn't able to say, such as: "I'm so glad to be here with you" and "I love you."

Over time, with consistent re-parenting of her inner-infant, Denise turned her insecure-attachment style into a secure-attachment style. She shifted the foundational misbelief that she was unlovable to the belief that she was profoundly lovable and worthy of that love. The dark hole of emptiness that had been with Denise since infancy—the hole where her foundational fears lived—began to fill up with warmth and light, the light of her inner-infant, her inner-child, and herself.

IT'S PHYSICAL

As we've discussed, your inner-infant has no autobiographical memories, so they have nothing to tell adult-you in words. Like all infants, they communicated through physical expressions—smiles, tensing, relaxing, and yes, crying. To feel what they feel, you must first regulate yourself, so you can be open to their needs. The following exercises can help you self-regulate:

1. Breathwork

    As we saw at the end of the last chapter, giving our attention to our breath is one of the best ways to regulate ourselves and prepare to meet our inner-infant. Our breath is consistent and automatic—we don't have to think about it. It is available to us whenever we need it. We can count on it. And whenever we want to—as described in Chapter 4's "Try This" section—we can control it to get us back to a neutral state more efficiently. If we are upset or feeling off kilter in any way, we can take long, deep breaths that slow our heart rate to calm and ground us (Heart Breathing, Ocean Breathing, or Earth Breathing). If (like Judy), we're distracted and unable to focus, we can take fast, powerful breaths to expel the extra energy and come back into our bodies (Fire Breathing).

In addition to following the written descriptions at the end of the last chapter, you might want to google "breathwork" to find videos that show you what each type of breath looks like in practice.

2. Rhythmic Activity

Early childhood research has found that rocking, gentle swinging, walking, and riding in a car all give babies a good safe feeling within their nervous system. (That's why new parents can often be seen driving their colicky babies around at night or putting them in their carriers atop a running dryer—supervised, of course.) These repetitive, predictable, rhythmic movements mimic a baby's feeling in the womb, the optimum environment for a baby's healthy development.

This feeling is something we don't grow out of. Physical movement can help us self-regulate at any age. So the next time you find yourself anxious or out of sorts, try walking, singing, dancing, drumming, swinging, or stretching. Any activity that is rhythmic, patterned, and predictable works.

3. Crying

The first time Denise looked into her inner-infant's eyes, adult-Denise began to cry. She hadn't cried in years. But with the release of those tears, her procedural memories were released from her subconscious. She felt a sudden burst of emotion surrounding the abandonment she'd experienced in infancy and childhood. Her tears flowed for weeks.

This is not unusual. Many of my clients cry when they first encounter their inner-infant. Crying is how babies communicate. It's a manifestation of pure emotion. It's a "language" we use throughout our lives when we can't verbally express ourselves. Crying is our body's natural emotional cleansing process. It helps us to self-regulate by releasing our stress, while also flooding our systems with the feel-good hormones of oxytocin and endorphins. Thus, crying is especially useful as you re-parent your inner-infant. It proved to be a breakthrough for Denise.

So, the next time you feel tears coming on do not hold them back. Welcome them and let them flow. See what they have to tell you and what they can help you to release.

ATTUNEMENT

Parenting at every age is about attuning to the child and letting that guide you in guiding them. Attunement is even more critical for this nonverbal stage of life. Since your inner-infant can't tell you what's wrong, it's up to adult-you to sense it.

As we've discussed, re-parenting isn't about negatively judging our parents for what they did or didn't do. If you're a parent now, think back to when your children were born. Most of us were young adults when we brought our infants home from the hospital. Most of us were inexperienced at caring for an infant and completely unknowledgeable of childhood development. Even when we do what we think is best (like Jim's and my decision to sleep train our babies), we don't always meet our infant's needs.

Re-parenting is simply going back and shoring up those areas where our parents or caregivers didn't or weren't able to give us what we needed as individual beings. Because the beliefs of inner-infant are foundational, the shifts you make by effectively re-parenting this stage are profound for your adult life and your ability to re-parent your inner-child at every other stage and phase.

TRY THIS: BABY YOURSELF

- Exercise 1 – Self-Regulate

    The next time you can't sleep, feel angry or anxious, or experience digestive issues, employ one of the techniques above to self-soothe and regulate. Do breathwork. Put on some music and sway. Take a walk. Or if you can, have a good cry.

    Note how you feel before the physical activity. Then, note how you feel afterward.

- Exercise 2 – Control or Regulation?

    Take some time to journal about your own infancy and early childhood. Did you grow up in a house filled with rules and expectations? Or did your parents help you to self-regulate? Where can you see their parenting style reflected in your life today—your self-image, your life choices, etc. Bring awareness to this as you re-parent your inner-infant, as well as the other stages of your inner-child.

6

RE-PARENTING YOUR INNER-TODDLER
(AGES 2-4)

Natalie was forty years old, newly divorced, and back in school to become a child psychologist when she came to me for help. She was having trouble focusing. When she was supposed to be studying, she'd often find herself staring off into space for hours instead, unaware that time had passed. Also she reported that sometimes when she was taking a test or even a pop quiz, her chest would tighten and her stomach would cramp so much that she couldn't pay attention to what she was doing. Consequently, she feared falling behind in school and being unable to earn her degree. Most recently, an episode of chest tightening and stomach cramps landed her in the emergency room, where she was diagnosed with a panic attack. That's when she decided she needed a therapist.

As we reviewed her childhood history, she informed me that she'd been sexually abused repeatedly by a family member when she was around three years old, though she had no memory of these incidents. She reported being in her twenties before—with input from another relative—she realized what had happened to her. She also told me that her parents divorced when she was a baby. Her father, whom she longed for, never showed up for scheduled visits, which made her feel rejected.

Her mother—whom she knew loved her—worked long hours to provide for the family. So her mom wasn't always there physically or emotionally for Natalie and her siblings. Natalie described her childhood as lonely. She shared with me that she decided to become a child psychologist to provide neglected and traumatized children the support they needed, support she hadn't received as a child.

As we've discussed, what we experience in our first three years of life not only creates but also sets in place the lens through which we view the world throughout our childhoods and into our adult years, each judgment and resulting behavior deepening the neural pathways that reinforce our beliefs. Research confirms that the attachment style we began developing in infancy (secure, insecure, insecure avoidant, insecure anxious, or disorganized) continues to form throughout our toddlerhood, and if our circumstances don't change, it settles in place before our fourth birthday. Human beings survive through sticking together and working together. How we relate to the world and people in it are fundamental to how we operate. So it makes sense that our brains become partial to an attachment style by toddlerhood.

What we can gather from Natalie's history is that infant-Natalie had no reliable adult to make her feel safe and help her to regulate her system. Her mother loved her and did what she could when she was available, but her mom could not be relied on. That another adult could sexually abuse her repeatedly—and her mom wasn't there to protect her—only served to cement this notion in toddler-Natalie's head.

Each time Natalie was molested, her body experienced pain she couldn't understand. Her body naturally reacted by tightening up and bracing, then pulling away or closing up in defensive positions. At three years old, Natalie didn't have a developed prefrontal neocortex, so she could not rationally process and recover from these assaults on her own. She certainly didn't have the vocabulary to tell her mom what happened when her mom was at home. Also, she didn't want to add to her mom's stress. So Natalie was left to deal with the fear and confusion on her own. Her toddler-brain did the only thing it could figure to do to survive—it dissociated from her body. (That's why Natalie had no memory of the assaults.)

When the passive parental neglect (avoidable or not) Natalie experienced in infancy was compounded by the trauma of abuse, the insecure-attachment style she developed in infancy evolved into an insecure-avoidant-attachment style, i.e., she trusted no one, no place felt secure. The clenching of her muscles (tightening in her chest and stomach cramps) and the dissociating she used to protect herself during these assaults became her body's go-to coping mechanisms whenever she felt stressed. At forty years old, her body was still using those techniques to respond to stress—though now triggered by being back at school and starting a new career.

The takeaway for you here is that what happened to you as a toddler is today informing how you move through the world, as well as the thought and behavior patterns that constitute your most stubborn fear loops. If your current self-image, relationships (professional and personal), and life patterns aren't what you want them to be, the solutions you seek most likely can be found by re-parenting your inner-toddler to a more secure-attachment style where needed.

STILL ATTACHED

As "toddler-you" (ages one to three) developed physically, intellectually, and socially, your world opened up. Able to crawl, walk, better grasp and manipulate objects, and verbally communicate (a little bit, anyway), toddler-you was gaining a sense of self and independence. However, though you had the ability to physically walk away from your parents or caregiver, emotionally you were still very dependent on and so connected to them. Toddler-you likely didn't let your parent out of your sight for long. You needed them to make you feel safe and regulated.

When my granddaughter was a toddler, I often took her to a playground in a nearby mall. Standing on the sidelines with the other caregivers (mostly moms), the toddlers all appeared so independent as they busily negotiated the tiny plastic slides, climbing structures, and each other. But if you stood there for a minute or two, it was no mystery which child belonged to which parent. Eventually, every single toddler would look up from play and search for their parent until they made eye contact. If the parent connected and smiled, most toddlers would visibly acknowledge that connection, express reassurance, and return to play. If the parent were distracted by their phone or looking after another child and missed their toddler's gaze, the toddler would become distressed. Once distressed, the child would stop what they were doing, go to their parent, and get the reassurance they needed with a touch or a quick hug. Then, off they'd go again.

All toddlers are innately driven to explore the world. At the same time, they're driven to survive and keep their systems regulated. At this stage of development, these two drives are in tension. The job of the toddler every moment of every day is to do their best to find their balance between independence and safety. To do this, they stay keenly attuned to their parents' moods and feelings. They monitor their parents' reactions in order to gauge what their own response should be, as well as to regulate themselves. I'm sure you've seen a toddler fall or hurt themselves and look to their parent to decide whether they should cry or not. How a parent (or caregiver) responds to a toddler's needs builds the toddler's life skills and gives the child information on how the world works, all of which informs their still developing attachment style.

Because their language is just emerging, toddlers remain more sensitive to moods and feelings than exact words. What their parents say doesn't matter as much as how the parent feels to the toddler when they say it. For instance, your parent may have told toddler-you to go play. But if your parent was nervous and anxious when they said it, toddler-you likely picked up on their anxiety and remained close by. Or if your parent tried to comfort toddler-you with the words, "I love you," but said those words with a scowl, toddler-you likely felt rejection more than love. If that became the norm during your toddlerhood, that rejection might have fed into your attachment style and caused you to carry that wound into adulthood.

WHAT TODDLER ATTACHMENT LOOKS LIKE

Researcher and developmental psychologist Mary Ainsworth developed an experiment called The Strange Situation, which allows us to see the various attachment styles in toddlers. The experiment begins with a mother and toddler entering an unfamiliar (strange) playroom. Mom encourages the toddler to play with some toys—and then she gets up and leaves the room. Most toddlers show stress once this happens by crying and crawling to the door. Still crying, they stare at the closed door waiting for their mom to return. When Mom re-enters the room after only a few minutes, the toddler's reaction reveals their attachment style—which is indicated by how well the toddler uses their mother's presence to calm down and regulate their own activated nervous system.

For the securely attached toddler, their mom's presence works quickly and efficiently. Typically, these children cry loudly when their mom leaves. But when she returns, they lift their hands and move toward her. When she picks them up, they press against her with their full body and head. They put their arms around her neck. They go for as much skin-to-skin contact as they can get. Typically within thirty seconds, these toddlers are calm and wanting to play with the toys again.

Insecurely or anxiously attached toddlers use their mother partially to calm down, but not quickly or efficiently. (This is the style Natalie had as an infant.) These toddlers also cry loudly when their mother leaves the room. They too lift their arms and move toward their mom when she returns. Once in her arms, however, they are unsure and so arch their backs and resist skin-to-skin contact. They also continue to cry. As the mother tries to comfort her toddler, the toddler gets angry and pushes her away. Mom becomes anxious because she doesn't know how to calm her child. The baby senses this, becomes anxious too, and so keeps crying. And on and on it goes.

For the insecure-avoidantly attached (the style Natalie adopted after the abuse) and for disorganized-attached toddlers, their mom's presence isn't all that helpful in regulating them. Insecure-avoidantly attached toddlers do not cry or fuss much when their mother leaves them alone in the room. They do stare at the door and wait seemingly patiently for their mom to return (signaling they still need their mother). They also typically engage in fake play with the toys. When their mom does come back, they show little emotion and do not move toward her to be held or picked up. As they continue their fake play, they do look up at her periodically to verify she's there. These toddlers have learned—most likely from their mom's behavior—to push their emotions down inside of them and not to fuss.

Disorganized-attached toddlers do cry when their mothers leave. But when the mother returns, they exhibit odd behaviors such as moving backwards or sideways toward her. Some move toward the wall. Others spin around and around. Still others collapse to the floor crying. These avoidant moves signal that these toddlers both need their mom and at the same time, are afraid of her. They don't know what to do.

DEVELOPMENT BUILDS ON DEVELOPMENT

During our toddler years, our brains grow to eighty percent of their adult size. We take in so much information that our brains prune themselves in our third year of life. This pruning clips off the neural pathways we don't use much, in order to give more energy and capacity to those we do use and to make room in our brains for the next developmental milestones. (This is the first of two such prunings in our lives, the second happening right before we enter adolescence.) The information and strategies we didn't use much in toddlerhood get wiped out. Those that were most common and helpful to us become the foundation of our thought processes moving forward.

Natalie had been primed from birth to push her feelings aside in favor of others' feelings. Natalie learned at an early age that her survival depended on her ability to sense her mother's stress level. To keep her mother from breaking down, Natalie intuited that she needed to be seen as a comfort to her mother, not another stressor. Later, she would employ the same strategy with her abuser. She learned she could prevent the pain by not fighting back. When a child does this, it actually lowers their stress and anxiety because it gives them a little control. It calms down the abuser, as well. Natalie did this to survive. She could not fight. She could not run (flight). She was three years old. All she could do was comply to survive. That's what she did.

Before she was four years old, Natalie's brain had pruned away any notion that the world was a safe place for her or that her feelings mattered—neither of those thoughts were helpful to toddler-Natalie. Her most used and driving belief was that the most dependable way to keep herself safe and regulated was to keep other people happy. Obviously, toddler-Natalie could not have verbally expressed any of these calculations. But just because we don't have the language to express what we've experienced or the conclusion that we draw from it, doesn't make those experiences and conclusions go away. Everything that had happened to infant- and toddler-Natalie was now integrated into the foundations of her nervous system, compounding her stress and raising her baseline for the level of neglect and abuse she'd tolerate as a child and as an adult.

Thus, it came as no surprise to me that beyond the issues with schooling that brought her to therapy, Natalie struggled to feel secure in relationships. Throughout her life, Natalie had longed for closeness. But people always seemed to let her down. The biggest frustration in Natalie's life was that she saw herself as the most trustworthy, helpful, loyal person she knew—and couldn't understand why others didn't reciprocate.

As the worldview Natalie developed early in life put up barriers to secure her from harm, unfortunately, it also took away her ability to engage in an intimate relationship with anyone. When you don't trust anyone, you can never fully be yourself. She navigated life by being a people pleaser. She was compliant when it came to authority figures, friends, and teachers. When it came to boyfriends, subconsciously, she relied heavily on her sex appeal. Because development builds on development, if Natalie wanted to change these patterns in her life now, she'd need to look back to those first three years of her life where the answers were.

THE RISE OF THE FALSE SELF

Even if your parents were not stressed, anxious, angry, or unavailable, things still happened to you in toddlerhood that likely caused a foundational misbelief and fear loop that's keeping you stuck now. Like most parents a generation ago and some parents today, yours probably believed (misbelieved) that toddlers are naturally rebellious and need to be reined in. They believed that because that's what our culture believes. We've all heard this stage of development referred to as "the terrible twos." We're taught parents need to teach their toddler to respect authority and behave. We're taught that when a two-year-old says "no" or throws a tantrum or insists on wearing snow boots in June, they're doing it to see how far they can push us and what they can get away with.

They are not. They aren't that clever. They don't yet have the brain power to scheme. They're simply trying out new skills, seeing "what happens if," feeling whatever emotion pops up, and doing their best to figure out how to be in the world.

As we've talked about, toddlers are still extremely dependent on their parents, and they're not wired to make their "survival source" their enemy. Also, no matter how loudly the parent yells at a toddler melting down in the grocery aisle, the child doesn't have the capacity to obey. They can't filter their own emotions, let alone their parent's. Toddlers don't have the abstract thinking (i.e., delayed gratification) necessary to prefer and then choose polite behavior. All they hear is the yelling. What they attune to is their parent's distress, which makes them more upset.

When your own parents tried to shut down your toddler-feelings, chances are you didn't miraculously leap ahead in your development and become able to self-regulate. If you learned anything from these interactions, it was—as soon as you were able—not to show your true feelings. Experience taught you that when you express what you feel, Mom or Dad gets angry or withdraws their presence, which rouses an innate fear in children.

As human beings, we're wired to need attachment more than to know who we are. Being our authentic selves doesn't matter so much when we feel threatened. Survival always comes first. But we weren't meant to live under the threat of pain, abandonment, or worse every day, all day long. It isn't a healthy state for anyone— especially not for children.

Children who feel threatened—whether growing up in an actual war zone or in a home where they fear the loss of their parents' love and approval—do not play, explore, act curious, or learn. They're too focused making sure they don't upset their survival source—their parent. Always on alert, they never get the opportunity to take the developmental step of experiencing their feelings in advance of learning what to do with them. Instead, they learn to mask true feelings and pretend they feel the way others want them to feel.

While such a strategy might get a person through a rough childhood, it can leave them confused and unable to successfully navigate adulthood. Not being able to know what you feel about anything ripens into not knowing who you are. When a difficult emotion (such as anger) does surface, adult-you doesn't know how to cope with it and so you find yourself reacting to it, exhibiting behaviors that aren't productive and that you may later regret. Then, you hate yourself for having that forbidden emotion at all and berate yourself as "bad."

The more emotions we decide not to feel, the more masks we put on and the further removed we become from living our authentic lives. The longer this goes on, the more difficult it can be to tap back into our real emotions and into our real selves. Because our false self is the only self we know, we are in danger of believing it's who we are. Driving all this is the fear we felt as toddlers. The fear that no one would love us if they knew the real us. In time, this becomes our foundational fear loop. Natalie's life and issues show this.

All human emotions have a purpose. They are not good or bad. Emotions give us information we need for living, navigating, and enjoying our lives. They are a cornerstone, a building block to secure attachment. Instead of being coerced into denying their emotions, toddlers need acceptance and then guidance in managing their feelings productively, so eventually they can self-regulate and come to know and trust themselves. When a toddler becomes overwhelmed (which happens a lot), they don't need a punishment they can't understand. They need their parents to comfort them and help with their feelings. Toddlers who are given the space to feel what they feel grow into adults who know what they feel, are unafraid of emotions, and are able to use their feelings effectively. I know this wasn't my experience as a toddler. It probably wasn't yours either.

Emotionally repressed toddlers grow into repressed adults. This is why we now have a population full of people with bottled-up anger, shame, depression, and a sense that something is wrong with them. Many adults today—maybe you included—suffer from depression, angry outbursts, and physical disease resulting from years of trying not to feel.

To become an emotionally healthy person with a secure attachment, your inner-toddler needs to be allowed to experience all of their emotions and come to view each as normal and useful. At this stage in a child's life, parents don't need to solve anything or come up with any big answers. They just have to be present and attuned to their toddler—allowing the child's nervous system to connect (attach) with theirs in order to regulate when needed. By experiencing this interaction as consistent, toddlers naturally begin to move toward self-regulation. It's an experiential learning process that's much more suited to a toddler's capabilities and so much more effective than verbal commands and punishment. You can give all this to your inner-toddler—and thus, to yourself—through re-parenting.

RE-PARENTING YOUR INNER-TODDLER

Re-parenting your inner-toddler means finding and healing whatever disrupted your ability to securely attach to your parent or caregiver. For some people—like Natalie—those might be issues like abandonment and trauma. For others, it's finding areas of more subtle repression. For all of us, re-parenting our inner-toddler comes down to allowing ourselves to be fully ourselves and experiencing that in safety and without judgment.

As the parent of your inner-toddler, your job is simply to hold space for your little one—to validate whatever they feel and allow them to attach to your energy to regulate themselves and find their balance. Through this process, you want to help your inner-toddler feel secure enough to take off their mask, so adult-you can finally take off yours.

When Natalie began re-parenting her inner-toddler, she wasn't so comfortable at the thought of meeting her three-year-old self. Unresolved trauma had caused Natalie to compartmentalize or repress much of her procedural memory—thus the dissociating and gut cramping. She was apprehensive thinking about what she might uncover.

Where we began with her—and where I recommend you always begin—is becoming present in your body. This is accomplished through using one or a combination of the breathing techniques we've talked about to calm the body's nervous system and bring it into the parasympathetic state (i.e., the rest-and-digest state). Once our body feels relaxed and safe, we can guide our minds to move inward and connect with the body.

When fully present in your adult body, you next need to check in and ensure you can welcome your inner-toddler. When Natalie connected to her body, she felt chest tightening and stomach cramping—the negatives of her inner-toddler. This signaled to us that she needed to do some more inner work before she could provide her inner-toddler with parental attitude that would be needed for a secure attachment.

She still felt resentful toward her three-year-old self. She said she was irritated at her toddler-self for being so difficult and needy at the time. She was angry at her for being disobedient, a burden to her mother, and always seeking attention. Because of our culture's negative view of toddler behavior, these feelings about the inner-toddler are not uncommon. However, because toddlers are so attuned to those around them and respond more to feelings than words—adult-you must be sure all negative feelings are resolved and you are in a loving headspace before calling on your inner-toddler.

To facilitate ease within adult-Natalie, allow her to trust in herself, and drop all that judgment she was laying on her inner-toddler's behavior, I began guiding her with statements like: "Notice how your breath naturally flows in and out." "Invite your mind to float along with your breath as it flows with ease." "Your body knows how to breathe. It breathes for you and knows what it's doing." "You can trust your body." You too can use such statements to give yourself confidence as you prepare yourself to meet your inner-toddler.

Once Natalie became comfortable, she was able to sit next to her inner-toddler. After a time, Natalie slowly moved toward connection. First, she and her inner-toddler looked into each other's eyes and breathed in sync. (I know it's only one body. But as you visualize and feel your inner-toddler, you likely will have the sensation of two nervous systems breathing.) Adult Natalie breathed more slowly and steadily in order to help three-year-old Natalie calm her nervous system.

In time, adult-Natalie was able to hold and comfort her inner-toddler. They snuggled, and toddler-Natalie got to feel what it was like to be comforted by an adult who was present for her. With repeated connections—adding kind words, trust, and full acceptance—a secure attachment grew. During those sessions, adult-Natalie experienced a calm in her chest and stomach.

As she got to know her inner-toddler, Natalie accepted that her people pleasing and dissociating were necessary coping mechanisms to get her through a traumatic childhood. She also realized they were hinderances now in her adult life. She saw that her insecure-avoidant-attachment style had been her baseline since the age of three, which explained why she chose to enter into relationships with people who were emotionally unavailable. They wouldn't demand intimacy from her, intimacy she didn't have the capacity to give at the time. Most of all, Natalie understood that if she were going to have the life and quality of relationships she desired, she needed to experience and establish a new baseline and a healthier, more secure attachment style.

Through re-parenting, adult-Natalie was able to feel and acknowledge the truth of what she'd lived through in those early years. She developed a new way of talking to herself. Instead of criticizing and shaming, her inner-voice now encouraged. Thanks to this work, Natalie was well on her way to moving away from the insecurity that made her behave in ways that were inauthentic to her and toward a more secure attachment to herself.

As you re-parent your inner-toddler, encourage yourself to be curious, ask questions, explore, and, most of all, be kind to toddler-you. Begin with breathing. Move to connection. And when the time is right and the relationship strong, give your inner-toddler the assurance they need that you are there with them always, close by, watching over them, and ready to refill their emotional cup when needed.

TRY THIS: WHAT DO YOU FEEL?
Toddlers are all about emotions. To get in touch with your inner-toddler, you must be able to identify what you feel. If you're not so good at that, don't worry. This exercise will help.

- Step 1 – Sit quietly and become aware of any sensations in your body.
- Step 2 – Do a body-scan from toe to head.

Give your attention to your feet. Feel their presence. Feel any sensations. Then do the same for your ankles. Your shins. Your knees. Your thighs. Your hips. Your stomach. Your chest. Arms. Hands. Neck. Head. Above your head. And back down to your heart. As you move through your body, notice your heart rate, your blood pressure, any tightness anywhere.

- Step 3 – Then, scan again.

    This time scan for any emotions you feel. If you feel something, name it. Notice how it feels.

- Step 4 – Talk to your emotion (out loud).

    Get curious—ask it what it's about, where it came from, what it has to tell you, etc.

- Step 5 – Then journal about and reflect on what you learned from this exercise.

7

RE-PARENTING YOUR INNER-SMALL-CHILD (AGES 4-7)

Chris had been suffering from daily migraines for six months. The prescribed medications were no longer effective, and the migraines now were so incapacitating that for hours every day he was unable to leave his bed. He'd had to quit his job and go on disability, which he felt ashamed of. Adding to that shame, he'd also gained a substantial amount of weight and was now on diabetes and high blood pressure medications. Only thirty years old, Chris felt he should be in peak physical form and in the prime of his life. He wanted to get married and have children. He saw his body as betraying him—and he didn't seem to be able to change things. By the time he made his way to my office, he said he felt like an old man and was questioning if he even wanted to live. He was in a full-blown depression.

As part of his intake process, I had Chris fill out an Adverse Childhood Experiences (ACE) questionnaire. It consists of ten questions about traumatic or negative experiences in childhood. Though migraines and childhood trauma might appear to be unrelated, several studies beginning in the 1990s, now called the ACE studies, have confirmed that adverse childhood experiences lead to dysfunction and many leading causes of death in adults.

During the study, researchers asked 17,000 patients ten simple yes-or-no questions about negative childhood experiences. For example: "Did a parent or other adult in the household often or very often... swear at you, insult you, put you down, humiliate you, or act in a way that made you afraid that you might be physically hurt?" Yes or no. These original ten questions became the ACE questionnaire. The study found that the higher a patient scored (the more "yes" answers they gave), the poorer their physical and emotional health was across their lifespan. Further studies and research have verified these results.

The study shocked the medical community. The conventional wisdom (which you still hear ad nauseam today) was kids are resilient, they "grow out of" any childhood trauma. But as in the research, most of my clients—and my own history—show the truth is much different. Children don't have the facility or the experience to process trauma fully. All a child can figure out to do with trauma is find a way to manage themselves through it—and often, that involves repressing the memory of it.

This, of course, affects how they develop mentally, physically, emotionally, and socially. Unless realized and processed, these outlooks and behaviors are carried right into adulthood—where they present as stubborn fear loops that keep us stuck in bad habits, bad situations, and bad relationships. Not surprisingly, carrying the burden of unresolved childhood trauma has been shown to lower life expectancy.

Chris scored eight out of ten on his ACE questionnaire. Obviously, he'd experienced a lot of trauma in his childhood and had carried it forward into adulthood. And like many clients with painful childhood memories, Chris didn't want to talk about it, even in therapy. He told me he didn't have much of a relationship with his father, but he and his mother had worked hard to forgive and forget. He liked to focus on the mom he had now—not on the drugged-out mom with violent boyfriends, not on the mom who often hit him and his younger sister.

So we started his therapy with a practice he felt safe with, focusing on his breath. This gave him—a client alienated from and angry with his body—a way to work toward bringing his mind and body back together. Once that connection was restored, his body and mind could work together to help Chris uncover and resolve his issues.

Using slow, deep breaths and body-scan meditations, eventually Chris felt his body's sensations again. And what he felt was a lot of fear—as if something or someone from the outside was going to attack him. I suggested he bring into his mind an imaginary support animal for protection. Most clients choose a dog or cat. Chris chose a shark—a great white one—which gave me some insight into the kind of waters he swam in as a child. As he spent time with his great white shark, he felt safer, more resourced, and more comfortable in his body. Chris still couldn't talk about his childhood yet—even to himself. But with his imaginary shark, he began to soothe the dissociative survival reaction that was disrupting his mind-body connection. In time and over several sessions, Chris's inner-five-year-old felt safe enough to appear.

FROM MEMORIES TO MISBELIEFS

When he came to my office, Chris was obviously suffering from deep feelings of unworthiness, which were fueling his depression and perhaps triggering those migraines, though that wasn't clear yet. So it was no surprise to me that one of the first of his inner-children to come to him was five.

Between the ages of four and seven, our language skills strengthen to the point we develop autobiographical memories—conscious memories in the form of stories, as opposed to the procedural (emotional/subconscious) memories of our infancy and toddlerhood. Also as young children, we learn about our world through imaginary stories and characters—animals who talk, magic things that happen. We believe everything we're told. This is the age of deep belief in the tooth fairy, the Easter Bunny, and Santa Claus. We also make things make sense, even when they don't. When presented with something we don't understand, we make up our own stories about why it is the way it is based on what we do understand. This kind of logic—child logic—combined with that willingness to believe is what makes it so much fun to hang out with children in this phase of development. It is also how children become stuck with misbeliefs that hold them hostage throughout their lives.

From the day he was born, Chris had only known a world that was uncertain and full of danger. He received no validation or guidance from either parent. Whenever Chris tried to assert himself, he was met with physical and verbal abuse from his mother and her boyfriend of the moment. The only attention Chris got was in the form of beatings—that's what he would remember and carry forward as he grew. A good day was when no one paid attention to him. He learned to survive by staying quiet and suppressing his emotions—most especially his anger.

Between preschool and second grade, our big developmental tasks include learning about ourselves, our feelings, and building our competencies—mostly through play. If you watch small children play, you see them work out various scenarios from the grown-up world they are witnessing and trying to make sense of. They play house. They make their stuffed animals fight. They dress up in costumes to try out different adult roles. They learn about their world by pretending.

Remember, our brains have just been pruned to make room for new neural connections. As young children, our brains are tuned to take in a broad spectrum of information. But because of our limited experience in the world, we often misinterpret some of what we take in—including our beliefs about who we are. If not questioned and reinterpreted, we take these misbeliefs into our next stage of development as autobiographical memories. And we build on them, just as we build on our attachment style.

As a small-child, Chris interpreted his mother's erratic behavior and cruelty toward him as something he was causing, not as her problem—a common thought process in children. From these early childhood memories, Chris formed the memory and misbelief that he was unworthy. It was a notion he'd carry into adulthood.

While our parents are still very central to our lives as small children, we also now know a world beyond them in pre-school and then elementary school. Developmentally, going off to school is a significant stage of life transition. With each new year and each new classroom, we're presented with a new set of expectations to fulfill and the potential to experience a different sense of ourselves—for better or worse.

Children in this age range are very interested in pleasing the authority figures in their lives—which consist mostly of their parents and teachers. They're driven to try to get it right. By the time we're five years old, we've figured out where we fit in our home environment and what to do to belong and survive. When we enter pre-school or school, we naturally apply what we know.

But remember the brain's hierarchy of learning—first, you must feel safe. Then, you must feel welcomed to belong. Then and only then are you free to learn. Thus, if the classroom expectations are similar to what a child experienced at home, that child feels safer faster, finds it easier to fit in, and feels secure enough to learn. Their energy is freed up to build the neural connections necessary to take on new tasks like following classroom rules, increasing language skills, and learning colors and numbers.

However, when classroom expectations deviate from the home environment, small children can struggle. They're unsure how to behave or what's expected of them. This can lead to getting in trouble without understanding why. In addition, the brains of these kids are so busy trying to satisfy the first two levels of the hierarchy that they don't always gain the security or have any brainpower left over to put toward learning. It's no wonder they become frustrated with school and believe they're "not smart" or just "not good" at school.

For Chris, school was a markedly different environment than home. For one thing, he had to listen to an adult—and in his experience, trusting adults was physically risky. There were rules he'd never before been exposed to and ways of behaving he was unfamiliar with. He wasn't able to just fade into the background, where he felt safest. Feeling unsafe and uncomfortable only added to the feelings of alienation and unworthiness he developed at home.

Think about your own early school years. What impression do you hold of pre-school, kindergarten, or first grade? How was your relationship with your teacher? Did you find it easy or difficult to go along with classroom operations and the expectations placed on you? Do you recognize the beginnings of how you started to think about yourself? Your talents? Your strengths?

Keep in mind, the memories we form in early childhood aren't always factual. They certainly don't contain the whole story—because we would have had no way of knowing that. But they play a big role in who we become. We form them honestly. They become our perspective, our outlook on life and on ourselves. And unless we've processed them as adults, they likely remain our perspective to this day.

Some people, like me, have absolutely no memories they can recall from early childhood due to early childhood trauma. I only know stories from what my mom and others have told me. These stories can feel real to me though and have become my own memories that I access and work with in a mind-body session.

Clients often ask, "How can I heal if I'm not sure what actually happened?" My answer is that we trust whatever memories come up for us from our perspective. When our mind and body are resourced and fully connected, that's when our brain can access and communicate with our past.

LABELING

Because we believe what we were told as small children, when parents or teachers label us—and most do because that's how they were raised or taught—it can be especially limiting. When a small child repeatedly hears themselves referred to as the smart one, the dumb one, the pretty one, the athletic one, the one who's good or bad at (fill in the blank), they take that label on as part of their identity. They believe that's who they are and don't question it. And don't be fooled, seemingly good labels given to you at this age can do just as much damage as seemingly bad ones.

Often these labels are reinforced through the expectations we intuit from the authority figures we want to please. As all children are, I was very aware of my mother's expectations. My mom had labels for each of us children that explained our roles in the family. She said she loved us all, but some of us were harder to love and made her life as our mom more painful—which is frightening and threatening to a small child. So little me paid big attention to everything she said and did my best to fulfill my role as "the good one." At the same time, my younger brother fulfilled his role as "the rebellious one."

These labels became our job in the family, our duty, our purpose—and eventually our identities. They determined our personalities, behaviors, and our futures. My brother "rebelled" in school and then in adult society. I conformed and became the peacemaker. We each became what we had been told and grew to believe we were. It would not be until I re-parented myself that I realized I was not a conformist at heart and had agency to be whoever I wanted to be.

Most poisonous to our lives is that through those labels we start to form and internalize beliefs about what we're capable of and what we're not. Once in school, we now have others to compare ourselves to. We see reflections of ourselves, begin to notice differences, and wonder if we are worthy, if we are enough. For the first time in our lives, we think things like: Bobby always gets the first spot in line because his last name is Adams and A is the first letter of the alphabet. Kimberly usually gets the most stars for completing her work and waiting for others to finish. Where do I fit in compared to others in my class?

THE BIG LABEL: GENDER

Perhaps the label that has the most profound effect on the trajectory of our lives—and one that is defined in our minds in this stage of development—is gender. Though your inner-child has likely heard a dialogue of gender since birth (and maybe even before), between the ages of four and seven, toddler-you starts to put your own language around it, understand the expectations of it more concretely, and connect behaviors with it.

Gender is a social construct—meaning the characteristics of it are decided by culture, not biology. Options for gender identity include man, woman, transgender man, transgender woman, non-binary, or a-gender (someone who doesn't claim a gender). Sex, on the other hand, is biological and physiological, with ninety-nine percent of humans born male or female, one percent born intersex. Sexual orientation options include heterosexual, homosexual, bisexual, transexual, asexual, and a-romantic (meaning you have no interest in romantic relationships), demisexual (meaning sexual connection must include emotional connection), pansexual (someone who is sexually attracted to all people), etc.

Today, a majority of people regard gender as being on a spectrum. However, if you're an adult today, chances are when you were a small child and throughout most of your formative years, gender was a binary thing—either male or female. And long before your fourth birthday, you were labeled one or the other, though your gender consciousness may still have been fluid at that young age. By the time you were seven, however, gender was likely embedded in the way you thought about yourself and what you thought was possible for you, whether or not you felt comfortable with your given label.

In an ideal world, children would be left to discover the right place for themselves along the gender spectrum. Each being allowed to express themselves in any way that felt right to them. For instance, those who identified as boys would feel free to express sadness by crying. They wouldn't give a second thought if they preferred tap dancing to football. Those who identified as girls could be angry if that's what they felt and could love trucks more than dolls without being labeled a "tomboy."

But here in reality, our parents and our greater society not only label us as boy or girl from a young age, but they also give us an entire menu of expectations to go with our gender—what our preferences should be, how we should feel, how we should dress, how we should behave, what we are capable of and what we're not, etc. A friend once told me that her mother's obstetrician would announce that the mother had either given birth to a "little dishwasher" or "a little soldier." Guess which gender belongs to which job title? I'm betting you had no trouble with that.

Remember when you were a small child, you took what the authority figures in your life said literally and believed it. So when a parent or teacher said "boys don't cry" or "girls don't yell" or when they suggested you play the flute or clarinet if you were a girl, the trumpet or drums if you were a boy—you got the message, and it became part of your unexamined belief system about yourself. If the expectation fit who you were, great. If not, you've spent a lifetime living with the discomfort of it, perhaps wondering what's wrong with you and why you can't just be "normal."

When you take a good look at how our society operates, you see how much of our world is defined along gender lines. You realize how having all these aspects of our lives defined for us before we have any agency over ourselves narrows us as individuals and as a society. The reality is that every human, no matter our gender, feels the same emotions and has the same emotional needs. So every human should be able to access those emotions, recognize their true needs, and know their true selves.

Again, this is not to place blame on our parents, teachers, or society at large but to bring awareness to how what happened to us as small children may be affecting us now. Examining this can help illuminate what we struggle with and point us to what might need to be re-parented.

SEXUAL ABUSE AND THE SMALL CHILD
Sadly and resulting in a host of consequences, it's in this developmental phase when sexual abuse is most likely to occur. Statistically,

children ages four to seven make up the majority of those treated in doctors' offices for physical and sexual abuse. One reason is because at this age, they can be physically overcome by adults. Just as significant, this age group is easily tricked and manipulated with instructions, such as: "Don't tell anyone or I'll hurt your family." Also, most small children know nothing about sex, so they're not even sure what happened to them. Lastly, there's more opportunity for abuse at this age. Unlike infants, small children are out in the world and so not as closely supervised by parents. They may spend six hours a day with another adult teacher or caregiver who becomes an abuser.

I remembered my perpetrator made me promise that I wouldn't tell anyone. So when I had to pick him out of a lineup, six-year-old me felt scared and bad—for him! In my skewed logic and my need to be "the good girl," I'd broken my promise to him, and breaking promises was "bad" behavior.

Considering the chaos in his home, I expected—and Chris confirmed—that he'd suffered repeated sexual assaults as a small child. His perpetrator threatened to hurt Chris's younger siblings if Chris told anyone. Chris felt responsible for his siblings' protection and safety. He'd already experienced the profound harm adults could do, so he took the threat seriously. Little-Chris worried constantly that the perpetrator would kill his siblings if he didn't act like a "man" and keep quiet.

Many of my clients who were sexually, physically, or emotionally abused during this young age, find within themselves a desire and curiosity to revisit their development in both their gender identity and their sexual orientation.

THE ORIGIN OF OUR ANGER

Even small children who feel physically safe and have a secure attachment to their parents find themselves in situations that frustrate or confuse them. After all, children this age don't have much control over their lives. They also don't have the experience or intellect to fully comprehend what's happening, why, and what it means. And while they do have a little more self-control than they did as a toddler, they're still more than a few decades away from having the full executive functioning needed for emotional restraint or to choose delayed gratification. In other words, they want what they want when they want it and don't understand why they shouldn't have it.

So naturally, when they are frustrated or upset about not getting their way or something else, they show their anger. And more often than not, the adults in their lives try to shut that anger down. They tell the small child that their anger is bad and unacceptable—because that's what they were told as children. They expect the small child to control themselves—which is developmentally close to impossible, unless the child fears the adult, and then it's not true self-direction but another emotional reaction. They punish the child for having the anger, thinking they're helping the small child to gain self-control. The result of this very common scenario in our society is that the small child learns to feel shame for feeling the way they do. Remember, a small child wants nothing more than to please their authority figures. When that adult tells them what they feel is bad, the child feels shame.

Further, these small children miss out on learning to trust that what they feel is real, exploring why they feel it, and then figuring out—with a trusted adult's guidance—a healthy way to resolve their uncomfortable feelings. But that's not how our society has evolved to operate, which is how we end up with so many adults with anger issues. Most of us have been stuffing our anger since we were young children.

I know for myself that when someone is angry at me, my go-to defense is to shut down and then ruminate for days afterward. I rarely if ever express anger directly toward another person—though I most certainly feel it. Such repressed anger does nasty things to our bodies. Chris's repressed anger turned into depression, weight gain, and eventually migraines.

Anger's purpose is not to hurt, harm, get revenge, or teach someone a lesson—those are negative places our reaction to anger goes when the anger is not tended to. Anger is a message to the person who is feeling angry. That person—whether four or ninety-four—needs to feel that anger in their body. Recognize the tightness, the clenching, the heat, cold, pulsing, and throbbing. It needs to be located and validated without judgment. Once that happens, we can set to work with curiosity toward understanding the anger. The goal is to get into a habit of using our anger to get to a beneficial truth, so we can eventually release the anger and move forward in our lives.

RE-PARENTING YOUR INNER-SMALL-CHILD

How your experiences as a small child are now affecting you as an adult may not be obvious to you. Or perhaps, like Chris—and frankly, me—your experiences may be so emotionally charged your brain keeps you from going there.

Re-parenting your inner-small-child is about finding and healing the misbeliefs and fear loops preventing you from being exactly who you are and loving yourself fully for it. The misbeliefs from this developmental phase typically express themselves as feelings of shame, unworthiness, not living up to expectations, and a general sense of not belonging. The fear loops created during this age range typically produce behaviors that can be connected to fears of rejection and abandonment. The anxiety and tension brought about by such issues can manifest as chronic pain, such as (but not limited to) headaches, shoulder issues, or backaches. They can also result in body-hatred, leading to disordered eating.

As you re-parent your inner-small-child, you want to look at what happened when you were between the ages of four and seven. Question the labels (gender, sexual orientation, and otherwise) that were imposed on you then. Look at any "shoulds" you live with today that may have their roots in your early childhood. If you did suffer sexual abuse, re-parenting is your opportunity to process that trauma with the support of your adult perspective, so small-child-you can feel safe in the world and be rid of any blame or shame. And of course, your inner-small-child also holds the key to so much of your automatic behaviors when it comes to anger—and for the majority of us, our go-to response to anger is to suppress it.

Parenting a small child is different from parenting a toddler or infant—though they still require encouragement in the form of kindness and love. So as you re-parent your inner-small-child, you not only want to give them that safe space and security, but you also want to show them they have some agency and control in their lives. That means making sure they know you're there to protect them if they come across a situation that's beyond their years to manage, while also allowing them to have their own perspective and make their own choices. Rather than saying this is the way it is, help inner-child-you to explore options, give them choices in their decision-making. Sit with your inner-small-child and see if they can come up with another option or choice that maybe adult-you didn't think about before. When our inner-small-child can do that, we disrupt old patterns enough to change our labels and "shoulds" where they first formed. We give ourselves the space to make new choices that reflect our true preferences.

Chris harbored deep-seated anger toward both his parents for not protecting him and for dismissing the past. If he brought up the past, they'd say things like, "I'm sorry, but that was so long ago. It's not healthy for you to continue being a victim." In one way or another, his parents would indicate to him that they felt he was weak and too sensitive. When they did this, that five-year-old boy inside Chris blamed himself for not being enough, not living up to their expectations. Adult-Chris expressed this sadness the only way most men in our society know how to express any emotion—anger at his parents and anger at himself.

So when his inner-five-year-old-self showed up in therapy, I invited Chris—with his shark by his side—to use the opportunity to give that child the validation he deserved. First, Chris simply listened to his five-year-old's pain. He felt it in his body. Then, I guided Chris in saying out loud to his inner-child, "Yes, that's right. You were right. Your anger is valid and true. I agree with you. I am your witness."

At the end of the session, adult Chris said with an exuberance I hadn't seen in him before, "I was right. I knew it. I was right." He also reported feeling respect for himself. Which made sense to me. When our feelings are validated, we are validated. We feel seen. From that session on, whenever Chris felt dismissed by his parents, he'd turn inward and validate his five-year-old inner-child. This calmed his nervous system, regulated him, and dissipated his anger so he could function.

After several sessions of re-parenting his inner-small-child, Chris had a dream in which he, as a small child, was sexually molested by a mysterious character. He believed his dream was a repressed memory. To honor and stand up for his inner-child, Chris decided to tell his family about the dream. They reacted like they always did by rejecting his story. In that moment though, curiously, Chris found their dismissal no longer mattered to him. He saw—and felt—that he'd spoken his truth and that was enough, he was enough.

After that incident, his migraines disappeared. Chris also found he was making decisions without obsessively second-guessing himself. He stopped seeking his mom's approval. Chris even let go of his resentment toward his parents. In time, he was able to forgive them. As his depression improved, Chris started to think about getting back to work, maybe training for a new career. Most importantly, for the first time in his life, he had the curiosity and wonder to explore his options and the possibilities for his life going forward.

Chris's story illustrates how re-parenting to heal repressed anger or any of the issues rooted in this time in development also releases shame and blame. Keeping a label we don't want affixed to ourselves is simply a response to a fear loop. We're afraid that being true to ourselves might result in our losing love—and the belonging that goes with it. But that is conditional love and should be lost.

We want to re-parent our inner-small-child (and all our inner-children) to experience and expect unconditional love, most especially from adult-us. We want them to know and be free to accept all of their feelings and emotions, including anger. We want them (and so us) to discover and realize their unique potential. In my practice, I've found that people who are able to re-parent their inner-small-child become more open and accepting of themselves, less judgmental. Because they are less stuck in the past, they feel hope for their future.

TRY THIS: MIRROR WORK
Use this exercise to take and get a good look at yourself—the real you, not the you the world expects you to be.

- Step 1 – Find a substantial mirror in your house.
    Your bathroom mirror will probably do.

- Step 2 – Look in it. Welcome your adult-self.
    Affirm what you see. Use specific affirmations if helpful.

- Step 3 – Now, welcome yourself as a small child between the ages of four and seven.

    - Look deeply into their/your face. Smile. Notice how your inner-small-child feels in your adult body. Breathe into it.
    - Ask what affirmations this inner-small-child might need. Breathe and listen.
    - Provide your inner-small-child with any affirmations they suggest, as well as affirmations to support their developmental phase, such as: "You are safe." "Your feelings are valid." "You can choose."
    - Offer your inner-small-child those affirmations along with your unconditional love.

- Step 4 – Don't look into a mirror for the rest of the day.

    - Carry your inner-small-child and the love you have for them with you as you go about your adult routines.

- Note any feelings that come up.

- Step 5 – Before bed, journal about your experience.

  - What did it feel like to be conscious of your inner-small-child? Emotionally and physically.
  - Write down what you learned about your inner-small-child. Did that provide any insights for adult-you?
  - How do you feel after a day of affirming your inner-small-child and giving yourself unconditional love?

If your inner-small-child does need re-parenting (and almost everyone's does), use what you've uncovered here to help you in that effort.

8

FROM MAKE-BELIEVE TO REALITY (AGES 8-11)

When we're around eight years old, our brain's neocortex (the cap around the inner and lower parts) is developing rapidly—priming us for more conceptual learning and more complex skills. For the next several years or so, we grow exponentially in our physical, social, intellectual, and emotional capabilities.

As our competencies increase, so do our responsibilities and our independence. Reason and logic enter our thought processes. We can now differentiate between fantasy and reality—slowly realizing for example that there's no such thing as Santa Claus or the tooth fairy. We develop our own interests, which we explore by joining sports teams, taking dance classes, becoming scouts, or playing an instrument. During my own grade-school years, I learned to play piano, to play board games, ride a bike, bake cookies, read a map, and I mastered all the rules for basketball, football, and baseball—all typical achievements for a kid between the ages of eight and eleven.

If you think back to your own grade-school years, you might remember that third grade was a lot different than second. You were no longer reading books with a few sentences per page, hoping to recognize words. You were now reading chapter books, comprehending what you read and gaining knowledge from it. Math, too, was different. The concepts were more abstract. You may have been introduced to multiplication tables and challenged with your first word problems. Additionally, you were able—and expected (with real-world consequences if you didn't)—to maintain your own desk and keep track of your belongings.

This is also when you began to label yourself according to what you perceive you were good or bad at or what other people said about you. "I'm athletic." "I can't spell." "I love science." "Math is impossible for me." Etc. How you grow to perceive yourself during this developmental stage sets the tone for what you believe (or misbelieve) yourself capable of, how you think about yourself, and how you treat yourself. Low self-esteem, constant self-doubt, fear of failure (and so fear of trying), or a paralyzing need for perfection in your life today are all signs that your inner-grade-schooler has some misbeliefs and fear loops in need of your adult attention now.

FITTING IN

As grade-school-us works at gaining new skills, we also look for reassurance and depend on approval to keep ourselves motivated. Because we now spend more time with peers than family, we start to care what our friends think about us, a trait that will strengthen with each passing year. For both better and worse, grade-school-us allows peer opinions to affect what we do and don't do, what we try and don't try, as well as how we feel about ourselves.

Most of us can remember being teased at this age and the emotional hurt that came with it. Usually, kids get teased about anything that makes them different—wearing glasses, our name, physical size or abilities, hair color, clothes, etc. Unless properly processed and put into perspective—which as grade-schoolers, we don't yet have the capacity or life experience to do—such rejection can leave deep emotional scars. I'm sure you can easily recall something you were teased about as a child, and you likely remain sensitive about that trait or event to this day.

My adult daughter Emma still becomes animated when she talks about being called out by a third-grade classmate for sucking her thumb. At eight years old, she'd already self-regulated this behavior to the privacy of our home, using her thumb only to fall asleep and calm herself when she was stressed or overly tired. However, one day at school, tired and stressed, she was staring out a window, when a boy pointed his finger at her and said, "Emma's sucking her thumb. Emma's a baby, sucking her thumb."

As adult-Emma tells the story, third-grade-her hadn't even been conscious her thumb was in her mouth. She remembers feeling embarrassed and humiliated. In that moment, she vowed never to feel that way again. And that's the last time she ever sucked her thumb. In that moment, she traded in thumb sucking for teeth grinding—a totally private behavior, though probably worse for her teeth.

It was a perfect solution to what a third-grader reasoned was the problem. At eight years old, Emma knew—as the other children in her class did—they were no longer babies and thumb sucking would ostracize her from her group. Emma's developing neocortex gave her the ability to recognize and care about the social judgment, decide what to do about it, and to do it—all emotions, awareness, and capabilities she would not have had just a few years prior.

Unfortunately, her neocortex didn't yet have the ability to help her properly frame the situation or realize thumb sucking wasn't the real problem, her anxiety was. She didn't have the brain power or life experience to comprehend there was an underlying cause to her need to self-soothe. At age eight, all she could do was react in the best way she knew to protect herself from what she saw as the harm. To fully manage and release herself from the emotional pain of this event, and to grow from it, third-grade-Emma—like all children in this developmental stage—needed an adult to guide her.

WHERE ADULTS FIT IN

Though eight-to-eleven-year-olds very much feel and react to peer pressure, the adults in their lives—parents and teachers—continue to hold the most sway over them, which provides real opportunities for us when it comes to re-parenting in this developmental stage.

While as grade-schoolers, we're inching toward independence, we remain very dependent on and so connected to our adults. We care what they think. We look to them for their approval and disapproval. We believe what they tell us and take to heart what they say about us. Most consequentially, we depend on them to help us understand the world we're now part of; to support our efforts as we try new things and strive to become skillful, independent beings; and to help us properly process the new situations and traumas that come our way. How our parents and teachers deliver that approval and guidance makes all the difference in the level of confidence and self-esteem we develop and take into our teen years and adulthood.

If we had neglectful parents who left it up to us to figure things out for ourselves during this developmental stage, chances are we became quite independent. But it's also likely that with no one around to witness our lives, encourage us, or explain things that happened to us, we formed a lot of misbeliefs about how the world works and about ourselves—misbeliefs that became fear loops that are still ruling our lives.

On the other end of the spectrum, if we had parents who oversaw our every move, made our choices for us, and stepped in before we were given a chance to manage a misstep or take on a challenge of our own, we likely became stunted in the areas of self-confidence and independence. Such children grow into teens and then adults who can't think for themselves because they've never been allowed to. Subsequently, they don't trust themselves to make a decision. They are gullible and easily persuadable—relying on others to tell them what to do (which can be dangerous). Again, misbeliefs about themselves and the world take hold and fear loops are formed.

The majority of us probably had parents somewhere in the middle of this spectrum, who were more naïve than purposefully neglectful or overbearing. Most parents want their children to become independent adults and do their best to make that happen, which usually means raising their children as they were raised. They have no knowledge of developmental phases and so don't know what their grade-schoolers need from them.

That's certainly the parent I was to Emma. If I'd been more attuned to her, her continued thumb sucking at age eight would have alerted me that she had anxiety. I could have made space for her to express her feelings about that—and then helped her to relieve whatever she felt pressure about. When she was teased at school, I could have guided her through processing those feelings. Instead, I assisted her in putting a Band-Aid on the issue by buying her a mouth guard. Looking back, I find it curious that neither I nor the dentist questioned why this eight-year-old was grinding her teeth in the first place.

PARENTAL MINDSET MATTERS

As my relationship with eight-year-old Emma shows, even when something feels like the right thing to do for the child, parents sometimes get it wrong. (If you are a parent now, you know this is all too true.) Recently I watched the movie *You Hurt My Feelings*, which explores the little lies we tell loved ones to avoid hurting their feelings. In one scene, the adult son complains to his mom about all the pressure he felt growing up. He accusingly yells (and I'm paraphrasing here), "You told me I was a talented writer. That I was special. You even bullied my English teacher until she changed my C grade to an A because I told you I deserved an A. I didn't deserve an A. I deserved a C."

His mom throws up her arms and replies, "Uh, you're welcome. I'm sorry I encouraged you!"

From the mom's perspective, she was supporting her son by showing confidence in his abilities. From her son's perspective, her confidence was misplaced. He hadn't yet earned the title of "talented writer" and knew it, so her calling him that only gave him stress. What he wanted and needed was for his mom to stop defining him by an outcome and accept that he was a work in progress, like all young adults.

In her book, *Mindset: The New Psychology of Success, How We Can*

Learn to Fulfill Our Potential, psychologist Carol S. Dweck describes two parental mindsets: The fixed mindset and the growth mindset. Parents with a fixed mindset praise achievement and outcome (like the mom in the movie). Parents with a growth mindset praise effort and process (which is what the son would have preferred). Though both mindsets come from well-meaning parents, each has very different effects on a child.

When parents focus on outcomes and only praise achievement, their children become afraid to fail and thus, afraid to explore and try new things. When these children do attempt something new, in addition to the challenge of it, they feel pressure to maintain their successful image to get that praise they so desperately want. Cortisol is released in response to that pressure and fear, which doesn't feel good. These children learn to work to please their parents—or others—not to achieve for themselves. You can only imagine how this dampens their potential during this eight-to-eleven-year-old developmental phase.

These children become conditioned to look for approval outside themselves, to let others decide their competence. They do not trust in their own judgment. Any good feelings they do have about themselves—and any release of the hormone dopamine—are dependent on other people's reactions to them. They never build self-esteem or self-confidence. Their whole lives become a struggle to prove they are good enough, which can lead to chronic anxiety, depression, and addiction disorders.

However, when parents focus on their child's effort and process, the child learns that there are rewards to simply trying and doing their best. This empowers them to take on new challenges without fearing outcomes. They feel in control of their lives and that feels good. Dopamine is released, making them want to continue to be curious, to take a chance, to reach their full potential as a human being. Over time, this builds self-esteem and self-confidence.

It's beneficial here to think about which type of mindset your parents, teachers, and other important adults had toward you as you were growing up. Your awareness here can help you identify areas that might need to be re-parented in your inner-grade-schooler—such as harsh self-judgment or fear of being wrong. And one more thing, when you do connect with your inner-grade-schooler, be sure to do so with a growth mindset.

YOUR INNER-GRADE-SCHOOLER

Even if we had the most attuned parents with the best intentions and the most expansive growth mindset (which no one does), they couldn't know everything we were up to or experiencing in our grade-school years. They certainly couldn't know how we were interpreting (or misinterpreting) those experiences. After all, for the first time, we were interacting with the world on our own terms, beyond the watchful eyes of the adults who cared for us and with all the vulnerability that brings with it.

What we can be sure of is that grade-school-us got a lot wrong. Thus, reconnecting with our grade-school-self and reviewing our reactions to the world around through their eyes can expose our most profound misbeliefs about ourselves, as well as the fear loops that keep us stuck in our patterns today.

Maria came to see me for severe depression—a condition she'd been treating with anti-depressant medications since she was a young adult in her twenties. Now in her forties and recently divorced, she was struggling, even though she was taking her medication. "I feel like a failure," Maria reported during her first visit with me.

In our sessions, Maria shared that she'd immigrated to the United States from Central America with her mother and three younger siblings when she was eleven. Her parents were divorced. She described her family as close-knit and religious. Being the oldest child, Maria—"gladly and with love," she said—had been her mother's little helper. Even before they came to the US, she took charge of her siblings when her mother was at work, which was most of the time. Her mother, she said, regarded her as a partner. Maria took great pride in the trust her mom placed in her.

Throughout her childhood, Maria dedicated herself to her family. Everything she did, she did through a lens of what they needed from her. She also excelled at school because (as she put it) she knew education was the way to a good job and her family needed money. During high school, she worked two jobs and gave her entire paycheck to her mom. Maria's mother was grateful for her daughter, always praising Maria for being so responsible and thanking her for her help. Maria idolized her mom. In her mind, her mom had sacrificed her life for her children. So Maria says she was happy to sacrifice her life for her mom.

A few years before Maria entered therapy, her mom died. Maria told me she was glad her mom wasn't alive to see the mess she'd made of her life. Maria was deeply ashamed of being depressed, being on anti-depressants, and worst of all, being divorced.

Note here that in all likelihood, Maria's mother never would have been disappointed in her daughter, no matter what. From everything Maria described about their relationship, her mother's approval and love was not conditional. That was a misbelief Maria formed herself in childhood. And understandably so. Most of the praise Maria received from her mother was for being responsible for the family. When her mom expressed appreciation for this, she had the best intentions. But because she was unaware of how her young daughter processed this praise, her mom didn't know Maria formed this misbelief, and so she wasn't able to help her daughter correct it. (In defense of parents everywhere, there's no guide out there to tell you how much to intervene or when attention becomes interference. Every child is unique, each with their own needs, each interpreting events in their own way.)

From the outside looking in, you might think someone like Maria who did so well with all her responsibilities as a child would move into adulthood with self-confidence to spare. However, her depressive state indicated to me that the many successes she did achieve throughout her life were propelled by her fear loop, not self-confidence. In her adult years, Maria had continued to work hard in her career and at home because she misbelieved approval and love needed to be earned.

So it only made sense that when she married, she invested her full self in pleasing her husband. As we explored this in therapy, she realized she'd transferred the relationship she'd had with her mother to her relationship with her husband. She made his happiness her happiness. Though she knew he was having affairs, she chose to ignore what she knew to be true. Instead, she became "embarrassed and angry" with herself. Ironically, it was her husband who filed for divorce, not her—further activating her fear loop and pushing her deeper into depression.

RE-PARENTING MARIA'S INNER-GRADE-SCHOOLER

Maria began the re-parenting process by first attending to her inner-five-year-old, who led her to her inner-two-year-old. Both needed assurance they were safe in their body and loved unconditionally. To provide this assurance, adult-Maria learned breathing exercises for self-regulating and techniques for connecting her mind and body. Once adult-Maria was calm, she was able to bring that presence to her inner-toddler and inner-young-child.

With that foundation established, Maria's inner-eight-year-old came to her. She, again, used self-regulation and a calming presence to connect with this inner-child. As her eight-year-old emerged, Maria felt a tense alertness throughout her body. Her eight-year-old-self confirmed that she didn't mind taking care of her siblings and that it meant everything when her mom praised her for her help. But she'd also let adult-Maria know that being responsible for running a household was a lot of pressure, and she didn't always know what to do, which made her anxious.

At the end of that first session with her inner-eight-year-old, adult-Maria and I discussed her niece and nephew, both of whom were currently eight years old and didn't have many responsibilities at home. After talking about how much she loves them, she admitted, "I do get angry that they don't take care of each other or their smaller siblings and cousins." This response told me that Maria was clearly stuck in the past, misbelieving that what had been asked of her in childhood was acceptable. I suggested Maria consider this from her niece's and nephew's perspectives. Perhaps they believed it was their parents' job to take care of the little ones and that kids should be kids.

With that, Maria broke down. She'd never considered that as a child she'd been forced by circumstances to take on responsibilities that were beyond what any child should be asked to do. For the first time, Maria could see it had been unfair of her mom (even if it had been necessary) to expect a grade-schooler to stand in for an adult. Her mother had treated her like an equal partner, which she was not. To relieve her mother's stress and keep her siblings safe and cared for, grade-school-Maria took on a persona of being in charge, of being responsible, of being competent. But it was a false persona. Every day, she was faking it. Every day, she was fearful something would happen that she couldn't handle, and she'd disappoint her mom and lose her love.

Faking your way through every day is hard at any age. But for grade-school-Maria, it created on-going anxiety and a hyper-alertness, both of which fed her misbeliefs about herself and her fear loop. Young Maria "reasoned" that if she worked harder and pleased others more, she could alleviate that anxiety and worry. It's a pattern that stayed with her throughout her life.

When her primary relationship was with her mother, this strategy worked okay because her mom would reward her with the gratitude and love she needed. As Maria matured, this approach also worked in school and in her career. Again, her loyalty and extreme effort were praised and rewarded—first with good grades and scholarships, and then with raises and promotions. Thus, her life experiences only reinforced her misbelief that the more she did and sacrificed, the more love and rewards she'd receive.

It only makes sense why Maria entered her marriage thinking the more effort she put into making her husband happy, the more he'd shower her with praise, gratitude, and the love she needed—as her mother had done. But Maria's husband was not her mom. He did not appreciate her effort. The behaviors that made her relationship with her mother harmonious, that made her successful in school, that made her a star at work did not transfer to her marriage relationship.

Maria could not have seen or understood that at the time. Sacrificing for the other was the only way she knew how to be in a relationship. And that had to change.

CHANGING COURSE

Using the re-parenting process, Maria explored the misbeliefs and fear loops that formed in her grade-school years. In session, inner-child-Maria shared with adult-Maria that she wasn't always okay with being her mom's partner. She felt anger, which she directed (misdirected) at her siblings for not appreciating all that she did for them. This was a revelation to adult-Maria. She would never have described herself as angry. However in retrospect, what her grade-school-self was telling her made a lot of sense.

Now that it was out there in the open, Maria realized she was angry. To this day, her sibling relationships were tense. She felt they asked a lot of her, were unappreciative, and that she was still "everybody's mother." As we looked back over her life, she identified moments when she exploded in anger without warning—taking everyone, including her, by surprise. She also realized her husband was the most frequent victim of these outbursts. With this revelation, Maria saw how her hidden anger kept her from being her authentic self, and thus from having truly intimate relationships. Her anger was harming her physical health as well. She suffered frequent bouts of shortness of breath, tight muscles, and muscle spasm—all signs her body was holding on to trauma.

Using this insight from her inner-grade-schooler, adult-Maria began to acknowledge and release her anger through simple exercises, such as Fire Breathing. She also wrote angry letters that were never sent to work through her emotions, come to terms with the reality of what had happened to her, and recognize her passive-aggressive tendencies, especially toward her siblings.

Maria took on a daily practice of re-parenting herself. She directed all her mothering skills toward herself and her inner-children. She validated for her grade-school-inner-child all she'd been through and all she'd felt. She used her time with me to work toward developing herself and her own interests (which she decided were yoga and dogs).

Slowly, with patience, kindness, and perseverance, Maria learned how to go inward, feel her anxiety, and regulate herself. To remedy her misdirected anger, adult-Maria set small boundaries with her siblings and practiced saying "no" to them, instead of getting angry with them. When she was with her siblings, she was careful to monitor her stress level and worked to let go of the need to be "everyone's mother." After family gatherings, she'd schedule "recovery time" to reset her cortisol and dopamine levels in her body.

As Maria grew stronger, she reported having a few emotionally hurtful but honest exchanges with her brothers and sisters. Instead of turning away and repressing her anger, she chose to work with her siblings through their feelings. She now trusted that they could handle her anger and she could handle theirs. Though difficult, these exchanges brought them closer as a family. The result was Maria was learning that she could be and deserved to be herself and be loved in every relationship she chose to enter.

COMPETENCE, CONFIDENCE, AND INDEPENDENCE

As we've discussed, from eight to eleven years of age, our brains are working hard to advance our competence, self-confidence, and independence. Anything that gets in our way—judgment, shame, fear, punishment—limits that progress and so limits our potential. Thus, this developmental stage is ripe with opportunities for misbeliefs to form, fear loops to be exercised, and behavior patterns to take hold. That's what makes your inner-grade-schooler a treasure trove of information when it comes to uncovering the thoughts and behaviors that are keeping you stuck today.

Nothing about re-parenting her inner-grade-schooler was easy for

Maria. She walked into my office many times and said, "I failed at my homework." You may find on your own re-parenting journey that reconnecting with your inner-eight-to-eleven-year-old is an emotional struggle, too. Here, I stress the only failure is not trying. That's as true for adult-you as it was for grade-school you.

Throughout Maria's re-parenting experience, it was two steps forward, one step back. But she kept showing up for her inner-child and for her adult-self. With time, that effort was enough for her to heal her wounds, release and correct her misbeliefs, see her true potential, and build a life worthy of her.

TRY THIS: BACK TO GRADE-SCHOOL YOU
This exercise is to help you reconnect to your grade-school self. To maybe uncover who you were, what your life was like, and what concerned you.

- Step 1– Pick one year—third, fourth, or fifth grade.
    Whichever is most vivid for you.

- Step 2 – In your mind—and in your journal—take yourself through one day in your life back then.
    Go from morning until night. Be as detailed as you can.

    - Did you fix your own breakfast or did your parent fix it for you?
    - Did you pack a lunch? If so, what did you pack?
    - Or did you eat at school?
    - If you walked to school, who did you walk with?
    - If you rode a bus, where was your bus stop? Who else waited with you?
    - If a parent drove you, why did they make that choice? What did you talk about on your way to school?
    - What were your teachers like?

- How did you respond to your teachers?
- What subject did you like best?
- What did you look forward to?
- What were you most afraid of?
- What did you do after school?
- Who did you have dinner with?
- What was your bedtime routine?

- Step 3 – Review what you wrote.

    Write down any events or emotions that stand out. Also note what you accomplished and what you were proud of.

- Step 4 – Take note of how your body feels...

    ... when you think about a certain event, a teacher, a coach, friends, and your parents.

- Step 5 – Note any patterns or beliefs that formed in this time.

    Have you brought any into your adult life? Are those beliefs true? Do they serve adult-you?

If your inner-grade-schooler does need re-parenting (and almost everyone's does), use what you've uncovered here to help you in that effort.

9

YOUR INNER-TWEEN (AGES 10-13)

A few years ago, my daughter Emma, thirty-one at the time, flew in from Texas to visit us for a week. During her stay, she invited a few of her childhood friends over to catch up. The young women gathered around our kitchen table talking and laughing—just as they had in high school. As I puttered around the kitchen, I smiled as I listened to their conversation, remembering many of the events they recounted.

Then Emma began talking about her daughter, Elena, who was visiting her dad for the summer. Emma told her friends that this year before Elena headed off, Emma had explained menstruation to Elena—what it was, what to expect, what to do, etc.—just in case Elena, who was ten at the time, started her period while she was away. According to Emma, Elena reacted to her concern and well-thought-out explanation with, "Eww, that's gross, Mom," which made everyone laugh.

I laughed too at first. Then my body tensed up, my face scowled, and my mind became hijacked by a fear loop. As Emma's friends jumped right in congratulating her on educating her daughter, I felt guilty that I hadn't been there for Emma, my own daughter. I hadn't explained anything to Emma about this next phase in her life and how to manage it. Or at least, I couldn't remember whether I had, so I assumed I hadn't.

I felt scared all of a sudden and wanted to hide. *Oh, no,* I thought, not even knowing why.

As I stared out the window and continued to listen, my daughter and her friends playfully one-upped each other with stories of how weird their moms acted when it came to menstruation. One of my daughter's friends said, "My mom was so uncomfortable, she pretended not to hear my questions and just walked away from me. Can you believe it!"

Another rolled her eyes as she said, "One day I went into my room and there were pads sitting on my bed. That was it. We never talked about it." Still another said her mom went so far as to take her to a doctor to avoid having a conversation with her at all.

Though they were all laughing and joking around, I intuited feelings of anger from them, as well. They were angry their mothers couldn't and didn't talk to them about such normal bodily function and such a significant life change—the onset of sexuality and slow march toward adulthood. Their mothers (including me) had left them to figure things out on their own. These young women vowed together that they would do better with their daughters. They would be like Emma, explain everything, and answer every question.

Part of me felt proud of Emma and her friends because I knew they were doing better for their daughters than their moms had done for them (again, including me). Another part of me wanted to run away and hide. That latter part took over. I left the kitchen and went into my bedroom. I sat on my bed in a pool of shame as I relived one embarrassing memory after another of avoiding Emma when she needed me because I'd been uncomfortable with this subject and unable to talk to her.

While my fear loop wanted me to stay stuck in that shame, I knew getting curious about my feelings would be a lot more productive. Why couldn't I talk to my daughter about her menstrual cycle? Why don't I remember my mother talking to me? Though I had no answers, because these questions and my feelings touched on areas of immaturity, embarrassment, and self-image around sexuality indicated to me that my inner-tween might need re-parenting.

UNCERTAIN TWEENS

Somewhere between the ages of ten and thirteen—our tween years—most human beings begin their transformation out of childhood and toward sexual maturity and adulthood. During this developmental phase, we experience physical changes—known as puberty—as well as intellectual, psychological, and social changes—known as adolescence. From start to finish, this transition typically takes about fifteen years or so, with most of us reaching full adulthood sometime in our mid-twenties.

In those first few years, physically we produce hormones, such as testosterone, estrogen, and progesterone. We grow taller, get hair in new places, and our reproductive organs become functional. Intellectually and emotionally, our brains enter a second "tuning and pruning" stage, like the one we experienced as toddlers. However this time, our brains prune away the neural pathways of childhood and tune up those we'll need to navigate adult life and propagate the species. So while we lose the ability to quickly recall every dinosaur classification (or endless facts about whatever interested us in childhood), our brain is shoring up pathways to increase our ability to focus, entertain abstract thoughts, and rationalize, among other skills. Socially and emotionally, we move toward becoming our own person, separate from our parents—though as tweens we are years away from individuation.

While full-fledged adulthood is a destination worthy of this decade-and-a-half-long journey, the journey itself is pretty rough for most of us—especially in these tween years. The body and brain we've known and relied on through childhood becomes unreliable in some very embarrassing, uncontrollable, and puzzling ways for a while. Think sweat that suddenly produces an offensive odor, penises that go erect without warning, or menstrual cycles that aren't yet on a cycle at all and surprise us at the worst times. Ironically, as our bodies become more awkward and untrustworthy, we begin to care about being attractive to others—though we don't fully comprehend why.

These first peculiar feelings of sexual attraction lead tweens to fantasize a lot. For instance, all of a sudden, we have huge celebrity crushes. These crushes, so typical at this age, allow us to explore our new feelings without the dangers or responsibilities of a real-life relationship. For those who do advance to "like-liking" a tween peer, even this relationship typically stays in the fantasy realm—meaning it's talked about with friends more than acted on. If the "couple" dates at all, they usually do so in a group with other tweens, with no true intimacies (physical or emotional) shared between them. Most tween relationships don't move beyond hand-holding. Famously short-lived, these unburdened forays into romantic love allow tweens to practice at relationships and lay the foundation for the neural connections (which continue to build throughout adolescence) for the more intimate and committed relationships in their future.

Note that this is a vulnerable, innocent age when it comes to feelings of attractiveness, sexuality, and self-worth. Peer-to-peer relationships are best and most healthy. Getting involved with a teenager who is further along in adolescence can put a tween in situations they aren't ready for, even if they think they are, and so can prove traumatizing and harm their development.

Making tween-hood even more difficult to navigate, each of us begins puberty and adolescence in our own time and moves through it at our own rate. When I think back on my own middle-school years, I clearly remember classes filled with all sizes of bodies. Some boys were as tall as grown men and had facial hair. Other boys looked much like they had in grade school. Some girls had grown long legs, had breasts and curving hips, and had their periods. Others of us were still waiting on that growth spurt and our periods, and had no need of a bra, not even a "training bra."

Whether we were ahead of our peers in our development or late bloomers, the one thing we all shared as tweens was feeling insecure and self-conscious. We weren't really teenagers, but we were no longer children either. Parts of us were stretching toward adulthood, while other parts remained firmly planted in childhood. (If you've parented a tween, you've likely seen this intellectual and emotional tension in real time.) As tweens, we were unsure of who we were in the moment and who we were becoming.

PRIMED FOR MISBELIEFS

So at a time in our lives when we want nothing more than to fit in and be accepted, we live in bodies we can't trust with brains we don't understand, in a world where we don't yet know the rules. Like my daughter and her friends, many of us had parents who were too embarrassed themselves to talk to us about what was happening to our bodies and brains at the onset of puberty and adolescence, what feelings we should anticipate, and how to navigate through these natural developments. And I think we can all agree middle-school health class didn't cover these topics very well either.

Add to this the mixed messages about sexuality and adulthood we received from our culture and religion—as well as half-truths we picked up from other "more knowledgeable" tweens—and it's no mystery why this life stage is ripe for forming misbeliefs and establishing fear loops, such as distorted body image, confused notions about sexual relationships and behaviors, and inaccurate ideas about who we are, what's expected of us, and what's possible for us. Misbeliefs around such subjects lead to complications in our adult lives and relationships. Additionally, because we are at the start of such a big developmental change, any trauma at this age—especially sexual—can have an outsized effect on our self-worth, self-image, and thus our confidence in ourselves.

My client Rosie came to me overwhelmed and exhausted. In her late twenties, Rosie was the mother of four children under the age of ten. The conservative Christian church she and her husband belonged to promoted the belief that children were a gift from God and motherhood was a woman's God-given calling. They also taught that child rearing was the mother's sole responsibility and that the father's only responsibility was to provide financially for the family.

After their third child was born, Rosie was diagnosed by a physician with postpartum depression. The doctor suggested she stop having children for a while and focus on her health. But Rosie and her husband rejected the diagnosis, ignored the doctor's advice, and chose instead to continue to be faithful to what they believed to be God's will. With the birth of their fourth child, Rosie's mental state deteriorated to the point that she was no longer able to safely carry out God's will and care for her children. All four were now staying with her sister. Rosie had agreed to therapy in the hope of getting well enough to resume her role as a mother.

In our first few sessions, Rosie shared she was engaged to her now husband, who is ten years her senior, shortly after she entered adolescence. They were married when she was seventeen. Her parents arranged the match—a traditional practice in their religious sect. Rosie remembered feeling happy with her parents' choice. She "knew" pleasing God meant having lots of children, and her husband-to-be would be a good provider. Over the decade or so she'd been married, Rosie reported being most proud that she conceived easily and her body responded well to pregnancy.

As we talked more, it became evident that Rosie was extraordinarily devoted to God. She told me Jesus was her best friend when she was a child. She loved knowing he was always with her. As a tween, Rosie enjoyed a few crushes on boys in her class. But the crush that remained most prominent in her mind was the one she had on Jesus. She loved to imagine him being as devoted to her as she was to him. She fantasized about spending her life with him and fulfilling her promise to him, which included having a house full of children.

Shortly after her marriage, Rosie was in a horrific car accident. She and a group of friends, also teenagers, were cruising around with the music up too loud, singing at the top of their lungs, and swerving the car in time with the music. Rosie was driving and lost control of the car. One of her friends died on impact. Most people would see this as a tragic accident, the sad and unintended result of teenage inexperience and risk-taking behavior. It was. I think we all get the shivers and count our lucky stars when we think back on the risks we took at that age.

But due to her religious beliefs, seventeen-year-old Rosie processed the accident and death of her friend as a punishment from God for "sinning"—meaning acting like a normal teenager and doing something she wanted to do, not something she'd been told to do. In Rosie's mind, venturing outside God's expectations for her had ended in an irreversible tragedy. From that moment forward, Rosie suppressed her developmentally appropriate trajectory toward individuation and retreated to a time in her life when things were clearer, where she wanted nothing more than to live for Jesus.

When I asked about interests beyond her husband and children, Rosie recalled liking art in middle school and high school. She smiled as she remembered various pieces she'd created and told me her teachers told her she had talent, which made her proud at the time. However, she quickly proclaimed that she'd felt even prouder when she got her first period in middle school—knowing it meant she could have children, which would please God. Like most women and girls in her church, Rosie believed her identity, self-worth, and meaning in life as a woman would come from being a mother. That belief was at the root of her tween fantasy, with none other than Jesus as her spouse. The certainty and safety of that fantasy comforted her most after her accident—so she clung to it.

For a time, it worked for her. But by baby number three, her beliefs about a life of accepting God's will and her lived experience weren't aligning. Despite her best efforts, the life path she believed she was born to fulfill—the one she'd fantasized about with Jesus—failed to materialize. Because she had never developed the independent thought needed to imagine another role for herself, she could not find fault with the belief, let alone change course. Thus, she put the blame on herself. Something had to be wrong with her. With that allegation came deep shame. She wasn't living up to God's plan for her, which activated her fear loop. With each pregnancy and each new baby to care for, that sense of failure deepened, resulting in debilitating post-partum depression.

FINDING YOUR INNER-TWEEN

Rosie's inability to move beyond her tween fantasies concerning adult life—and stemming from her beliefs—was extreme and had extreme consequences for her and her family. While most of us might not be so obviously attached to beliefs we held about adulthood in our tweens, the majority of us likely do continue to hold on to remnants of those beliefs, and they keep us stuck in areas of our life now. Often these beliefs center around what we think is required of an adult, how our adult relationships should operate, and who we need to be (both physically and socially) to be accepted by others. When we try to apply these tween beliefs to adulthood, we end up putting our energy into superficial areas that don't matter and ignoring what really does matter—leaving us embarrassed, shamed, and confused in one area or another of our adult world, just as we were as tweens.

Unresolved embarrassment and shame over my lingering confusion around my body and how I (as an evangelical Christian at that time) was supposed to feel about sex are what held me back from counseling my children as they moved toward maturity. Embarrassment and shame also prevented Rosie from admitting she needed help. These backward-looking emotions keep us tied to beliefs we formed in tweenhood before we had any life experience or facts. Such beliefs prevent us from seeing and accepting our current reality as it is, our adult selves as we are, and however we feel about sex as right for us. Moreover, because they keep us from knowing, accepting, and being who we authentically are—instead of some tween-idealization of who we should be—they stop us from achieving true intimacy with others and with ourselves, keeping us from the fulfilling relationships we desire.

Issues that stem from misbeliefs formed in our inner-tween usually present as issues around body image, negative patterns in relationships, and discomfort surrounding sexuality. For instance, while its normal for tweens to be pre-occupied with their looks (after all, their bodies are going through profound but awkward changes at the same time they want to fit in with their peers), how many of us carry this obsession into adulthood? We continue to hold ourselves to some cultural standard for appearance that no one can achieve without airbrushing—and we beat ourselves up when we don't achieve it. We cling to the misbelief that if only we were better looking, lost twenty pounds, were taller or shorter, had straighter or curlier hair that people would like us better and we'd be more successful in love and life. That's how tweens think. As adults, we know better intellectually. Yet that doesn't keep us from jumping on that misbelief's fear loop and investing our energy, time, and money to fabricate a face or body to meet some made-up ideal. Whether we succeed or not, the cosmetic and fashion industries make sure chasing the "look" is a never-ending quest, and so our tween misbelief puts us back on that fear loop with our constant companion shame.

Even a securely attached person fantasizes, experiences confusion, and feels insecure in their tween years. But as they progress through adolescence and reach maturity, they grow into their own person who knows, accepts, and can manage the realities of adulthood. Understanding what's happening to us and having our questions answered accurately during this developmental phase can make living through our tweens less stressful and help us reach adulthood with an accurate sense of self. If we didn't get this when we were tweens, we can give it to ourselves now through re-parenting.

RE-PARENTING YOUR INNER-TWEEN

Luckily, because tweens are just at the start of their transition to adulthood, their parents remain their most trusted sources for information and comfort—though their friend groups are gaining in importance.

Parents who attune to their tween and stay open to them without judgment are well positioned to defuse misbeliefs before they form, help them to self-regulate, and reassure their tween that their feelings and struggles are normal—that they are okay and will be okay. Adult-us has the same advantages with our inner-tween.

Issues with body image, negative patterns in your relationships, discomfort with sexuality, and persistent guilt that you're not living up to expectations are all signs your inner-tween has some misbeliefs that need your attention. Note also that if you experienced any life disrupters as you entered adolescence—such as your parents getting divorced, a beloved grandparent or parent dying, a big move, being bullied or being a bully, or any kind of sexual incident (traumatic or not) that left you confused—you'll want to revisit your inner-tween.

At such a vulnerable stage in life—with our body and brain in flux, with new feelings and sensations coming at us—misinterpretations should be expected. Unexamined and unchallenged misinterpretations morph into misbeliefs that follow us into adulthood. At this age, we simply don't have the experience to put life events into perspective. For instance, due to the sexual assault I'd experienced at six years old, I had several incidents in my tween years when I froze and let an older teen boy do whatever he wanted to me. Since my childhood assault was never discussed in my house, tween-me had no idea this freeze response was a natural protective reaction related to my childhood assault—and something I could have expected and saved myself from if an adult would have helped me process the earlier incident. Instead, I carried great guilt about these occurrences throughout my life. I blamed myself for them. This negatively affected my view of my sexuality and my self-worth throughout much of my adulthood, until I re-parented my inner-tween in therapy.

Because of the restrictive world Rosie grew up in and continued to live in as an adult, Rosie's misbeliefs and fear loops were particularly engrained in her—stunting her mental, intellectual, and emotional growth. Being part of a culture where her thoughts, decisions, and life were determined for her, Rosie never developed an authentic sense of self, which a person needs to become an adult. The one time she'd gone against expectation and acted in a developmentally typical way ended in a tragedy (the car accident) and added to her shame. No one ever explained to her that she was more than a womb and could have goals beyond motherhood. In Rosie's culture, autonomy and individuation weren't encouraged—especially not for women.

Rosie shared with me that with each pregnancy her mood lifted, and she was able to be a mother to all her children. But immediately after delivery, she'd sink into a depression. With each consecutive post-partum period, that depression became deeper and lasted longer. Since her mind could not yet fathom the fault to be her belief system (that would be blaming God), she'd concluded that she was defective, adding to the severity of her depression. In her mind, having her children taken from her was the last blow. Thus, her breakdown. Her conscious mind may have been telling her to have more kids for God, but her body and subconscious were rebelling. Somewhere in her body, Rosie knew there was more to her and for her than motherhood.

In our sessions, we turned to Rosie's inner-children—focusing mostly on her inner-tween—to help her untangle past experiences and her reactions to them. We started by grounding Rosie's imaginative mind in her body. Through breathwork and body-scan meditations, Rosie regulated herself and brought herself into the present moment. I then explained how her mind can lie to her and imagine things that aren't true—but that her body cannot lie to her. If she takes the time to feel what it has to say, her body will always tell her the truth because her body is real.

This simple concept enabled Rosie to stop reacting to disturbing thoughts and in time, self-regulate whenever anything upsetting entered her mind. It also empowered her to appreciate her body as more than a baby-making machine. She found her body spoke to her through emotions and sensations. And one of the first things it had to say was she was angry.

Maybe for the first time in her life, Rosie understood that she'd not been given a choice to pursue anything other than motherhood. Feelings she'd repressed since adolescence flooded into her consciousness—where she was finally able to feel them. Rosie described feeling split down the middle, as if she had two separate parts of herself living within the same body.

To help her bring those parts back together, Rosie reached out to her inner-tween. As they connected, adult-Rosie immediately saw the artist she'd been in middle school—fearless about creating, proud of her talent. Adult-Rosie assured her inner-tween this was a safe space, that she supported her, and they could talk about anything she wanted. Her inner-tween told adult-Rosie of her struggle. She feared that both being an artist and having pride in it was going against God and her family. Her inner-tween said she felt she had no choice but to live up to her church's expectations. Tween-Rosie said that she tried to talk herself into accepting this future and be happy about it, but she was also angry that she'd have to give up this art that was hers alone. This expression from her inner-tween finally allowed adult-Rosie to feel that anger too.

As you've seen in previous chapters, anger is a commonly suppressed emotion in our inner-children—because it results from lack of understanding and lack of control, two conditions of childhood. For inner-tweens, a lot of their anger evolves from the increasing pressure to conform to societal norms, especially to the gender roles of our culture. Tween girls are often expected to give up their tomboy ways and begin acting like young ladies. Tween boys can be teased if they're emotionally sensitive or don't like sports. In other words, this is when our culture asks us to start denying our authentic self and repress our authentic feelings in order to meet a standard and fit in. No one asks us if that's okay with us. Once again, we may comply, but our body holds on to that innate human desire to be who we are. It's only a matter of time until those repressed feelings make themselves known one way or another—and it's usually with anger, at least at first.

When a parent acknowledges their tween's anger (or anger at any age), validates it, and helps their kid work through it, the anger dissipates, the root cause is revealed. Thus, those causes can be dealt with openly, and the struggles that repressed anger would have caused in adulthood never materialize. But in our culture, we consider anger unacceptable and discourage its expression. In my more than two decades as a therapist, fully 100 percent of my clients have needed to re-parent themselves to process repressed anger. While I'm thankful they're able to do it, a lot of pain in their lives could have been avoided if they'd been permitted to feel and understand their emotions in the first place.

As Rosie gave her inner-tween space to be with her anger, she was able to come to terms with the grief and sadness at losing so much of herself. Tween-Rosie admitted to adult-Rosie that while getting her first period was thrilling, it was also frightening. At twelve years old, she could only imagine what the responsibilities of motherhood would be and what being a wife would require from her. She didn't feel up to it and didn't know that she ever would. (The car accident a few years later only added to her feelings of incompetency.) And no one was providing the details she needed to calm those fears. Compounding her anxiety was the thought of Jesus being disappointed in her because of her inadequacies.

With tween-Rosie's insights, adult-Rosie could finally see why real-life motherhood had paralyzed her. As her infants became toddlers, they developed their own personalities. Sometimes they expressed anger—as toddlers do. Rosie regarded any rebelliousness of theirs as the result of her poor mothering skills. She worried for their salvation and was ashamed of herself for not being able to take good care of their souls.

By bringing these fears into her consciousness, Rosie removed them from her fear loop. Now, we could examine them rationally for their veracity. I explained to her that anger in toddlers is not only appropriate but developmentally necessary. So her baby's anger was in reality a positive reflection on her parenting. Her children were secure enough to demonstrate their anger. To assist their development further, it was her job now as their parent to validate that anger—so they learn to correctly identify their emotion for themselves—and then coach them in working through it and managing it productively.

I let her know that when an adult takes a child's anger personally and reacts to it by ignoring it or punishing the child into suppressing it, that child becomes an adult who doesn't know what to do with this emotion—which can lead to a wide variety of unhealthy expressions of it. Rosie immediately recognized herself as such an adult. We discussed that the job of a good parent isn't to make children conform but to help them become their best selves.

Adult-Rosie used these lessons to re-parent her inner-tween. She validated tween-Rosie's fear of the future, as well as her anger over having to conform to her family's and church's expectations. Adult-Rosie also let her inner-tween know that she'd mature into her responsibilities and that wasn't a worry she needed to take on now. Adult-Rosie explained that the fantasies tween-Rosie entertained about marriage and motherhood were age-appropriate and to be enjoyed—but they are not real life and so she should keep her mind open.

By being a parent to her inner-tween, Rosie grew in her understanding of her adult-self, as well as in her confidence that she had the skills needed to be a good parent. In time, she left her tween fantasy of perfection behind. She stopped seeing the world and herself through the lens of good vs. bad. Instead, she accepted herself as a whole person. She accepted that she would make mistakes—and so would her children. She learned to repair ruptures in relationships and recover from mistakes, and so she was able to guide her children in doing the same. Last but far from least, she started confidently making decisions and asking for help when she needed it.

However, in our months of work together, Rosie never came fully into her own. She insisted Jesus was beside her at every session. When she spoke up for herself, she considered her "voice" to be that of the Holy Spirit. Wherever her strength came from, the important thing is she was able to tell her husband, family, and church that she wouldn't be having more children in the near future. She enrolled herself in attachment-based parenting classes to educate herself further on child-development—so she'd know what behavior to expect from her children, the importance of each behavior, and how best to respond to it to promote healthy development. She and her husband hired a nanny. And slowly, Rosie reunited with her children. First, her two youngest, an infant and toddler, returned home. Once they were settled into a routine, the two oldest joined them.

Rosie is never going to leave her church community. But now at least, she picks and chooses Bible verses that support her autonomy rather than crush it. Because of re-parenting her inner-tween, she's living a life that's realistic and manageable. Through this process, she's also attained parenting skills that not only serve to keep her healthy but will benefit her children through their development as well.

YOUR INNER-TWEEN NEEDS YOU

There's a reason so many popular movies and novels revolve around characters on the brink of puberty and adolescence. It's a dramatic time in life, full of confusing but often (looking back, anyway) humorous events. The adult biology advancing on our childhood bodies is both exciting and frightening, welcome and unwelcome. So much about us is changing in these years. At the same time, all of a sudden, we're too self-conscious to ask questions about it. All of it is beyond our control, leaving us feeling out of control.

We all have horror stories from this period in our lives, and so these movies and novels provide a cathartic release of pent-up emotions along with relief that we were not alone. We've all been through it, and we've all survived into adulthood.

No one gets out of tween-hood without some misbeliefs and fear loops that follow them into adulthood. Your inner-tween needs you to ask those questions they were too self-conscious to ask and to give them factual answers, to let them know that they are just fine the way they are. And you need your inner-tween to reveal to you what your misbeliefs are, where they came from, and how your thinking can be healthier for you as you move forward in life. Your inner-tween is calling you. Answer.

TRY THIS: BACK TO THE FUTURE
Take a moment to explore your inner-tween.

- Step 1 – Journal about what tween-you imagined your adult life would be like and what your lived reality is today.

    - Are there any areas in your current life that you feel disappointed in because you're not meeting the expectation you had for yourself? Your relationships? Your occupation? Your appearance? Your level of wealth?
    - Are there any parts of your life where you feel guilty about not meeting that expectation?
    - Is there any part of your life where that fantasy or expectation you have of yourself prevents you from enjoying your life as it is?

- Step 2 – Review your answers.
    Look for areas where re-parenting your inner-tween may prove useful to you.

10

YOUR INNER-ADOLESCENT (AGES 14-26)

When a friend of mine took her two-year-old for a wellness check, the pediatrician explained that toddlerhood and adolescence would be the two most dangerous times in her child's life. While that's a lot to spring on a young parent, the pediatrician had a point. Both these developmental stages are times of budding independence enhanced by increased capabilities and made riskier by the limits of life experience.

Somewhere around our second birthday, we realize we're separate beings from our parents. About that same time, we find we've become pretty good walkers—though still unsteady and ignorant of the experiences we'll be walking into. That, however, doesn't stop us from striking out on our own to explore the world and to discover what we can do in it. Though toddlers—unlike teenagers—regularly look back to make sure their parents are watching and keeping them safe.

By the time we reach adolescence, our brains are telling us we know enough to be our own source of security. We don't. But that doesn't stop our developmental programming from making us want out from under our parents' gaze. We feel driven to no longer be a reflection of them but to individuate—to be who we are (even though we have no idea who that is). So we use this returned need for independence not to explore the greater world but to explore ourselves this time, to figure out who we are and where we fit.

Having already gone through adolescence yourself, you know this is a crooked journey with many wrong turns being part of the process. Like the toddler's walking, the intellectual and reasoning capabilities teen-us needs to achieve individuation—while increasing—are not totally there yet and won't be until we're in our mid-twenties.

In truth, most people won't even reach full individuation in their mid-twenties or ever, at least not completely. Re-parenting our inner-adolescent now, however, gives us the chance to revisit this last leg on our journey to adulthood and figure out where we're still bound to others' expectations for us and the misbeliefs and fear loops that keep us there.

THE ADOLESCENT BRAIN

Since you came into existence, your mind and body have been evolving toward your becoming an independent adult with the physical and mental maturity necessary to care for yourself, as well as create and nurture the next generation. In adolescence—from around fourteen to twenty-six years of age (each of us enters and completes this phase in our own time)—identity and relationships become the major tools you use to get there.

Throughout this period, your body gains an adult physique and comes into full sexuality. You are both fertile and have a sex drive you must learn to manage. Luckily, at the same time, your brain's frontal lobes are getting closer to becoming fully operational, increasing executive brain functions that weren't available to you as a child—such as reasoning, judgment, impulse control, self-awareness, and all the other mental capacities we associate with maturity.

In the first several years of adolescence—throughout high school for most of us—these functions are spotty. Sometimes your new neural pathways fire, sometimes they miss. That's why teenagers can be so confounding to adults; one minute they're making a well-considered decision and the next, they're doing something rash or even dangerous. With each passing year, these executive functions become more reliable and so adolescent-us becomes more reliable. This is why a twenty-year-old-you was so much more pleasant to be around than fifteen-year-old-you.

The fact that our teen brains are inconsistent doesn't stop teen-us from insisting on depending on those thought processes and discounting the advice of our more experienced parents and other adults. Should teen-us decide we need advice, we typically turn to peers, whose brains are in similar condition as ours and whose life experience is just as limited. While this might seem like bad design, biologically and socially it makes sense. The only way to strengthen the neural pathways to our executive functioning—and make them the ones our brains choose to use first—is to use them. In the early years of adolescence, this leads to a lot of uninformed reasoning and bad choices with real consequences. However, we do learn from our mistakes and mature because of them.

Mistakes are the hallmark of this developmental stage and our experiencing the consequences of them enables our psycho-social development. Bad decisions teach us to make good ones—which is how we gain competence and the self-confidence to individuate. If this process doesn't happen—if a parent is always stepping in to prevent our failure and its consequences—neural pathways to mature thinking remain weak, our brain doesn't learn, our development gets stunted, and full individuation doesn't happen.

If you think back to your own adolescence, you can probably trace this learning process most clearly through your relationships with your peers. As we all know, peer relationships take priority in this developmental phase. Teens are known for trying out different friend groups and trying on different roles within those groups. And because our parents no longer choose our relationships and the situations we get ourselves into, we're forced to ask ourselves questions like: How do we allow others to treat us? Where do we fit? What do we value? Teen-us can't help but compare ourselves to others, as we work toward discovering who we are.

As we move further into adolescence, we move out of the "group dating" of our tweens and yearn for more serious, romantic, and even sexual relationships. Typically, we experiment with these one-to-one relationships in our high-school years and enter more committed, longer lasting relationships in our late teens and early twenties. However, it's perfectly normal not to have an exclusive relationship at all until sometime in our twenties—everyone is different.

Whenever they happen and however many we have, these intense, intimate relationships push our buttons, test us, and reveal us to ourselves in ways friendships can't. When processed well and with self-awareness, the hardships and heartbreak that typically accompany adolescent- and young-adult-romances provide the lessons that build the neural pathways needed to sustain a life-partner relationship as an adult.

IN OUR OWN WAY

However, processing any disappointment well and with clear-eyed self-awareness is an impossible order for a teenager or young adult who carries unresolved attachment issues, trauma, and misbeliefs and fear loops from their childhood. Whether we're managing friendships, navigating a new romance, or trying to get ourselves to school on time, everything we are and have been goes into the seemingly "independent" decisions and action we are learning to make as adolescents.

As in any phase of development, adolescent-us can't help but see everything from the vantage of where we are and what we know. Naturally, the neural pathways we depend on to judge situations and decide how to behave are the product of the totality of our lived experience up to this point in our lives and are filtered through that lens. Children who come to adolescence more secure in themselves—and with the neural hardware to support that—are better prepared to tackle the difficulties of this phase with resilience, accept and learn from their errors, and progress toward individuation. Those who've been conditioned in one way or another to look outside themselves for answers have a much tougher time reaching this important developmental goal because they don't yet have the necessary neural structures to identify their misbeliefs and situations with clarity.

If we developed an insecure-attachment style in childhood and never attended to it, we, of course, bring that style and worldview into the friendships and romantic entanglements we have as teenagers and young adults. Though outwardly insecure-teen-us may be rejecting our parents, inwardly our attachment system is still telling us how to think and behave. Our insecure style is then reflected in the people teen-us chooses to surround ourselves with. As we know, while our attachment style served to make our world functional and allowed us to survive as children, in adolescence and adulthood, these unhealthy styles seed the misbeliefs that keep us in our fear loops.

All insecure attachments cause us to look for validation from an outside source, making us emotionally dependent on others and thus vulnerable, especially as teenagers. For instance, if you developed an insecure-anxious-attachment style as a baby, teen-you probably chose friends and later romantic interests who you see as heroes and who you need to make you feel worthy. If you developed an insecure-avoidant-attachment style, teen-you probably looked for people who need you and in exchange will admire you. Insecurely attached teens change to fit the needs of others in exchange for a sense of belonging. As you can imagine, this is a set up for agreeing to risky behaviors—like drug use, crime, or unprotected sex. Taking it a step further, insecure attachment can lead to a lifelong pattern of co-dependent relationships, which land us in a cycle of abusive relationships, causing more trauma and keeping us stuck.

Securely attached teens, on the other hand, come into adolescence with an underlying emotional security and an internal sense of worth that supports them as they make their way to independence. They still struggle through their teenage years and make their share of mistakes.

But because their self-worth is internalized, they look to relationships for connection, not validation. Thus, they tend to make healthier, more productive choices to begin with. When they do find themselves with the wrong crowd or person, they are better able to recognize why it's not right for them and extricate themselves. They don't look to a group or another person for their identity. As you can imagine, entering this period of psycho-social growth with a sense of self makes it easier to discover who you are becoming and what decisions and behaviors best support that. Though securely attached teens do (like all teens) turn to their friends before their parents, they aren't afraid to ask their parents for help when they get in over their heads. They know—because it's been their experience since infancy—that their parents will help them without judgment and guide them in solving their problem or repairing their mistakes.

Most of us, of course, don't come to adolescence and the work of individuation secure in ourselves and with no life events that need re-parenting. But most of us don't come to this phase of life completely insecure either (though we may have yet to consciously repair our insecure-attachment style). Most of us are a mixed bag—able to individuate successfully in some areas of our lives and not so well in others. For instance, you may have followed your own desires when it came to your choice of spouse, but you're still working in the field your parents encouraged you to choose rather than the field that most interested you.

The work of individuation comes down to disentangling authentic you completely from the you who is in constant reaction to outside influence, even if that influence is loving. If you're an adult who feels like you live for everyone else; if you continue to negatively compare yourself to others; if you look to culture, religion, or another person for your opinions; your inner-adolescent still has some untangling to do and individuation to achieve.

This is where re-parenting your inner-adolescent becomes invaluable. The adolescent brain has more self-awareness than the childhood brain. Thus, the consequences of their decisions and actions are easier for them to show adult-us, revealing the misbeliefs and fear loops that have their roots in other stages of our development. Once identified, any harms or confusion can be re-parented and healed in their proper developmental stage. Then with our more secure attachment in place, our inner-adolescent can fully individuate, and we can become the adult we're meant to be.

RE-PARENTING YOUR INNER-ADOLESCENT

Though as teenagers we discount our parents during adolescence, how our parents managed us through this phase and throughout our entire childhoods—as we've discussed—is integral to our success in individuating and becoming full-fledge adults. As teenage-us makes the change from childhood to adulthood, our parents also need to be making a change from the authoritarian who rules our lives to more of a supporting role. Though our teen attention is on everything but our family of origin, it's imperative our parents stay attuned to teenage-us—to know what we're thinking, what we're feeling, what we're experiencing, and who we're associating with. Just as imperative, they must let teen-us make our decisions and feel and heal the consequences of them—while at the same time, being there to supply guidance when asked for or when it's a matter of safety. That's a big ask of our parents and a tough balance to pull off. Few parents do it well. None do it without error. All of this is why re-parenting your inner-adolescent can be so productive.

Twenty-four-year-old Grace came to my office reporting she was dissociating throughout the day, had foggy thinking, and was having trouble finding a direction in life. Under her own volition, she'd moved out of her childhood home about a year earlier and into a house with trusted friends she'd had since childhood. She was enrolled at a local college full time. Her father was supporting her financially while she finished school. She told me she'd been in an abusive relationship throughout high school but had broken it off a year or so after graduation. She hadn't dated since and wasn't really interested in a new relationship with anyone. She wanted to focus on herself and getting her life in order.

From all outward appearances, Grace seemed to be in a developmentally appropriate place for an older adolescent. She appeared more self-aware, self-motivated, and self-assured than most twenty-somethings I saw in my practice. On her own, she'd competently dealt with serious issues in her life already. Yet, the dissociation and foggy brain she complained of were signs that something within her still lingered unhealed.

Diving a little deeper into her high-school relationship, she said her boyfriend was physically and emotionally abusive—nearly killing her a few times, though she'd kept that to herself. Like most abusers, his insecurities made him controlling, as well. He monitored who she saw and where she went. He broke her phone more than once to isolate her from her friends. Grace expressed that she hoped therapy would help her to understand her reaction to his abuse. She didn't understand why she didn't fight back. Whenever things got tense, she said she froze (dissociated). She described it as floating above the situation and watching everything happen, separate from it and unable to intervene. More to the point, she couldn't understand why even now—with that boyfriend well out of the picture—she continued to dissociate when she wasn't in any danger. She felt like she was observing her life and unable to become part of it.

To help her find her answers, our next few sessions focused on Grace's childhood. Grace's mother had left the family when Grace was entering adolescence, leaving Grace in the care of her father. When Grace was little, she adored her father, though he worked long hours and was rarely home. When he was home, he was either reading or on the phone with clients. His way of parenting Grace had always been to set high expectations for her and do everything in his power to ensure she met them—a style her mother had complied with. Though loving in his way, he was strict about who Grace's friends were, what she wore, and what extra-curricular activities she participated in. Grace learned early in life that her responsibility was to do as she was told—and that making the honor roll and winning awards would make her father happy and get his attention, at least for a moment. The few times in childhood that she did assert herself or cross her father, he expressed great disappointment in her and withdrew from her. To Grace, the rejection was never worth the self-expression. So she did her best to do what he wanted and win as many accolades as possible.

Having a docile mother and a father whose love could not be counted on, baby-Grace naturally developed an insecure-avoidant-attachment style that was reinforced throughout her childhood. She learned early in life she had to perform to secure what she needed to survive. When those performances went against her own desires, she learned to dissociate from her feelings and do what was necessary to win her primary caregiver's approval and care.

It made sense to me that Grace had experienced abusive control in her life long before her teenage years. The abusive boyfriend was merely an extension of her relationship with her father. Though her father had never been physically abusive, the boyfriend's need to control was familiar to Grace—it's what she knew love to be. So she had no weapon against it. To her, control seemed a normal part of a loving relationship.

I'm not saying that Grace's father didn't love her. He may very well have loved her unconditionally and control was the only way he knew to parent her. But the result was that Grace learned that love is about control, it's conditional, and it can't be depended on. While that may have been a protective and necessary misbelief in her childhood, as a teenager, it put her in danger in her choice of relationships. And as an older adolescent, nearing adulthood, it was preventing her from individuating and trusting in herself enough to allow for an intimate connection to anyone or anything.

Impressively, by breaking up with the boyfriend, moving out of her father's house, and forming her own support group with her housemates, Grace had already taken huge steps to free herself from the control of others and advance toward her own individuation. Now that she'd taken care of the outside forces keeping her from authenticity, she needed to turn inward through re-parenting to dissolve the misbeliefs and fear loops still keeping her bound to her childhood thought processes.

As always, we started the re-parenting process with breathwork. As Grace became comfortable, regulated, and attuned to her body, she sensed the need to support her inner-teenager and re-parent her through the abusive relationship. Upon their meeting, teenage-Grace explained that she knew her boyfriend was abusive, but he had some great qualities, too. He was a lot of fun. He really loved her—and she liked that. She admitted he also scared her sometimes, and she feared for her life. She was ashamed to be in such a relationship and ashamed for not knowing how to get out of it.

Twenty-four-year-old Grace—acting as her own parent—told her inner-teenager not to blame herself. She told her she didn't deserve to be treated that way. She told her she was strong at her core. And adult-Grace said she believed that teen-Grace did know what to do. Grace encouraged her teenage self to stop listening to the voices of others, to get still enough to hear herself, and to love herself enough to listen to her own guidance. The beauty in this interaction is the parent-Grace did not tell teen-Grace what to do. Adult-Grace offered support and encouraged teen-Grace to believe in herself, which is what parents—and re-parents of adolescents and inner-adolescents—need to do.

When Grace emerged from that session, she reported feeling stronger and more grounded in herself than she had before. As she strengthened her belief in herself over the next several months, Grace slowly and competently re-parented her inner-children from infancy through the tween years—examining the trauma and repairing misbeliefs, but also learning to accept herself exactly as she was. Through this work, each of her inner-children found their voice, shared their own dreams, and became secure in adult-Grace's unconditional love for them, for herself.

With her "littles" healed, Grace had the foundation she needed to re-parent her adolescent-self to full individuation. By the end of our time together, Grace had found her adult voice and herself. She recognized that she'd confused control with love—and why that was. She gained more awareness around what she wanted and deserved in a partner. And she set boundaries with her father, who continued to try to control her with threats of cutting her off financially.

COMING INTO OUR OWN

Grace was in a pretty good place when she first entered therapy. I believe she was on her way to individuation on her own. Therapy and re-parenting, however, served to better define that journey for her, making the real hurdles visible to her, and thus, allowing her to reach adulthood with much more clarity, confidence, and self-awareness. In addition, the re-parenting process gave her a tool she could return to whenever she felt stuck in her life or found herself dissociating. It will do the same for you.

Adolescence is a potent period in our lives. Like no other developmental phase, re-parenting your inner-adolescent requires you to take a look at every stage of your life to uncover the forces that have stealthily kept you from knowing and accepting yourself. Further, your inner-adolescent holds the key to releasing the guilt that has kept you a prisoner of others' expectations. Through re-parenting teen-you, adult-you becomes free to be who you are—to know your own values, to have your own dreams, and to be confident enough in yourself to act on them. What else is there.

TRY THIS: YOUR RELATIONSHIP HISTORY

Because so much of our search for self happens in the relationships we choose, it can be instructive to create a timeline of significant relationships throughout your adolescence and early adulthood to look for any patterns.

- Step 1 – Make a relationship list.

    List all significant relationships outside your family of origin (friendships, romances, partnerships, mentors) you had from ages fourteen to thirty.

- Step 2 – Sketch out a timeline that includes all these relationships, noting:

    - The person's name.
    - Their relationship to you.
    - The date the relationships started and how.
    - What attracted you to this person?
    - If the relationship ended, the date it ended and the reason it ended.

- Step 3 – Study the timeline.

    - Note any patterns you see. Such as:

        - What kind of person are you attracted to for friendships? For romantic partnerships? What traits are most prevalent across the timeline?
        - Is there a recurring theme around when you enter or exit relationships? A misbelief you are acting on?

    - What do those patterns tell you about yourself?
    - Do your relationships reflect your attachment style?
    - Do you see an arc of personal growth over the years?
    - Can you identify an issue that keeps you from connecting with others in the way you want to?

- Step 4 – Don't do anything right away with your answers and observations.

Sit with them. Think on them. And as you relate to people in your life going forward, keep them in your awareness. If you choose to re-parent your inner-adolescent, use this timeline to bring a deeper understanding to your adolescent-self.

11

RE-PARENTING: A JOB THAT NEVER ENDS

While writing this book, I received a letter from my sister and brother-in-law asking if my husband, Jim, and I might reconsider our relationship with Jesus and return to church. Jim and I figured their request was in reaction to Jim having been recently diagnosed with cancer. They expressed concern for our souls and suggested two books that might help us find our way back to God.

I seethed as I read their words. How dare they. Jim's diagnosis was still new to us. We hadn't yet had time to absorb the shock of it. My sister and brother-in-law knew all that. They also knew it had been around four years since Jim and I thoughtfully left the church we'd spent most of our lives in and its radical brand of charismatic Christianity. We had no intention of returning to what we'd come to see as a false belief system and social structure that had encouraged our most self-destructive misbeliefs and fear loops.

As I handed the letter to Jim, I was more than angry. I was enraged. My stomach was in knots. I felt nauseous. Both signals to me that something deep-seated had been triggered by the letter. So I chose not to respond to the letter in my current emotional state. I decided to sit with my feelings until I felt clear on the source of and reason for my emotional reaction.

A few days later, I came out of a deep sleep in a twilight state, half-dreaming. Running through my mind were memories of me in the first decade of my marriage going to ridiculous—and frankly, unwelcome—lengths to get Jim's family to accept me as part of their family. I replayed the way I'd asked his mom to join us to see a movie or a play. I winced as I saw myself inviting her to go on vacation with us. I thought about all the time and effort I put into arranging playdates between our children and their cousins—an effort that Jim's brothers and their spouses never reciprocated. My mind then played a greatest hits countdown of my many over-the-top contributions to Jim's family get-togethers and holiday meals.

Still in a dream state, I felt his family's rejection of me all over again. (In their defense, my actions were excessive and they'd asked for none of it.) But at that time, I thought (misbelieved) that I had to be "the caring daughter-in-law" to get them to like me. So that's who I became. In reality, the over-zealousness of my false persona served only to stoke their discomfort around me. Right on cue, I felt the rejection and hate I carried for myself at that time. A loop of phrases ran through my head: "You were such a stupid idiot." "You're such an embarrassment." I remembered how often throughout my life I'd wanted to curl up in a ball and disappear.

However, as I came into full consciousness that morning, I wasn't immobilized by those thoughts, as I once would have been. The misbelief that I needed to be someone I wasn't in order to be accepted had been re-parented and healed in therapy long ago. I now both accepted and loved myself—and through that I enjoyed the true connection with others I'd been so hungry for when I was younger.

Yet, still in my bed, the shame of my former self was lingering in my mind. Try as I might, I could not push that discomfort away. So I got curious about it. Why after decades had those memories about Jim's family come to me anyway? Why was I still able to conjure the emotions around something that happened so long ago, something I believed I'd healed? I believed my sister's letter was stirring these memories and emotions. I believed it had more to tell me than was written on the page.

The need for re-parenting doesn't stop simply because we've already met with all our inner-children or because we've left therapy. The re-parenting process is a tool to be used throughout our lives, whenever we feel confused, triggered, or stuck. As I laid there in bed that morning, I was confused, triggered, and stuck. To gain the clarity and understanding that would release whatever in me was calling for my attention and give me the healing obviously needed, I did as I always do in such situations. I returned to re-parenting.

P.A.R.E.N.T.

To help my own clients take advantage of the re-parenting process whenever they need it, I developed an acronym to guide them step-by-step—P.A.R.E.N.T.

- P-ause whatever you're doing.
- A-ccept your inner-child with open arms.
- R-eside with your inner-child.
- E-xpress your inner-child's pain.
- N-urture your inner-child.
- T-rust that your body will heal itself.

Using this acronym that morning, I PAUSED by getting out of bed, sitting in a comfortable chair, and coming into my body with some calming breathwork. Once fully in my body, I held out my hands, palms up, to signal to my inner-child that I was open to her and ready to ACCEPT her. Within moments, I felt the presence of my inner-teenager—which surprised me a little. My fear of rejection and inability to connect with others—which I believed was what my twilight dream had been about—was a wound that formed in me long before adolescence. Thus, I was even more curious as to what she had to tell me. I made room for her to RESIDE within me by placing my hands on my chest and allowing myself to feel her throughout my body.

I asked if she was okay. She told me she was anxious. I told her I was sorry and here to help her. Through tears, she said she loved church more than anything. But in the last few years, she'd felt like an imposter there. "I think about things I know I shouldn't. I can't seem to help it. I want to be 'pure and holy' like my friends. I act like I am. I try to be good, but I'm not. And God knows it. I'm so ashamed."

With that, I took the next step of EXPRESSING her pain in my own body. I felt my stomach tying itself into knots. I also felt enveloped by the sadness of what those lies had her misbelieving about herself. I, of course, knew she was referring to our church's teaching that we should not only keep ourselves chaste until marriage but also have no sexual desires or fantasies until then. An impossible and ridiculous ask of any human being—made even more impossible because my inner-teenager had been left by her church and the adults in her life to figure out her budding sexuality for herself. Not surprisingly given what her church preached, she'd concluded (and now misbelieved) that something was terribly wrong with her and that her feelings were unusual, sinful, even evil.

Without hesitation and with total clarity, I put my hands on my heart and NURTURED my inner-teen. In my mind's eye, I took her hand and said, "Sexual thoughts and feelings are natural and to be expected for someone your age. They aren't evil. Everyone has them, even 'holy and pure' people. Not having them would be unusual." I explained that these feelings are part of our biology. They're a physical drive, like hunger and thirst that can't be denied. However, I explained, acting on our sex drive, of course, can result in a host of consequences, so we do need to learn to manage it and only act on it when it's right for us. I added, "But there's never anything wrong with feeling what you feel."

I then made sure she understood there was no way she could have known any of this on her own. An adult should have been there to guide her through this time in her life with facts, not judgment. I told her I was sorry no one had been there for her but reassured her that I was here for her now. Adult-me felt my inner-teen relax.

THE LAST STEP: TRUST

As my inner-teen receded, I still didn't understand what her issues and my twilight reveries about my in-laws had to do with my reaction to my sister's letter. Nevertheless, I moved on to the last step in the re-parenting process—TRUSTING myself and my body to heal whatever needed healing.

I stayed quiet. I thought about my relationship with my sister. I was a quiet kid who longed to belong but never seemed to—except when I was with my sister. She was a full ten years older than me but included me in everything she and her friends did. After our family moved from Hawaii to California, it was my sister who would walk across the field from her high school every day to check on me at my elementary school, knowing I was scared and feeling awkward. She was who introduced our dysfunctional and isolated family to charismatic Christianity when I was ten years old. The church brought structure to our lives and much needed community. My parents stopped fighting. I had a ready-made group of friends my own age—something I'd never had. In years to come, I'd realize how damaging the church's strictures were to my life and growth as a human being. But in those early years, it was my earthly salvation.

Trying to find my way in the world with an insecure attachment complicated by an early trauma, I struggled with self-image and self-worth throughout my childhood and into adulthood. But my sister's attention to me and genuine love of me always made me feel special and cared for. When my sister married, she chose sixteen-year-old me as her maid of honor. Afterward, both she and her husband continued to include me in their life. They took me camping, taught me to water-ski, and let me ride on the back of their motorcycle. They did the same for my children.

To this day, whenever I picture my sister, I see her with her arms stretched out for me. She took care of me when I couldn't take care of myself. She loved me when I couldn't love myself—when I spent my days mired in shame, unable to keep up the persona of "pure and godly" teenager or "dutiful-Christian" daughter-in-law.

Ah-ha! I finally saw it. When her letter came, I was in a raw and vulnerable place due to Jim's diagnosis. I'd allowed its message to set off old fear loops around judgment, which is why I was so triggered and angry, and underneath that, hurt. But my inner-teen helped me see that adult-me was no longer a person who became a puddle in the face of judgment. Faced with the letter, with memories that brought up shame, faced with my inner-teen's struggles—through it all—I'd maintained confidence in myself, in who I was and what I'm capable of. I chose curiosity and compassion over reaction and beating myself up. Without hesitation, I shared this belief in myself with my inner-teen, giving her the gift of believing in herself. Through re-parenting her, adult-me let go even more of the harshest judgment of all—self-judgment. I'd shown myself that I could take care of me. That was the truth I'd found here. To make sure I embraced it, I repeated it out loud five times.

In addition, by helping my inner-teen to self-regulate, adult-me had self-regulated. From that neutral stance, I now saw my sister's letter had come from an authentic place of caring—like everything she does. I also saw how much my sister and her husband deserved my gratitude, not my anger.

The letter I wrote back turned into a long-overdue thank you. Line by line, I acknowledged all they had done for me over the years. I let them know that their support and attention had played a large role in me eventually being able to love myself and to become the self-assured person I am today. I also thanked them for their current concern for me and let them know that Jim now had a solid treatment plan we felt confident in. The contents of this letter were a much truer representation of me and how I want to show up in my life for the people I love than a note written in anger and self-pity.

RE-PARENTING FOR LIFE

Re-parenting my inner-teenager changed my relationship with my sister. For the first time in my life, I related to her as adult-me, fully responsible for myself. She no longer needs to be my caregiver. She can just be herself. That's a different way for us to relate to each other. So there are some kinks and tensions that need to be worked through. But I now know that it's through that work that intimacy is created.

Re-parenting my inner-teenager also revalidated and strengthened my relationship to myself. Thanks to my inner-teen, I now understand more than ever that I belong to me first—and from that vantage, I'm in a more solid position to reach out and connect with others.

Once we start the re-parenting process, we never know where it will take us or what we'll learn about ourselves. We have to be open and trust in the process and ourselves. What we can be sure of is our inner-children will expose old wounds our minds have tried to protect us from and our bodies have held for years. They will reveal our misbeliefs and fear loops, bringing them into our consciousness whenever we ask. There, adult-us can examine them and bring them into alignment with reality, as well as our chosen values and intentions. Through the re-parenting process, we integrate our past with our present to become a whole person. We replace self-judgment with appreciation for where we've been and the positive truth of who we are now. We live with clarity, curiosity, and belief in ourselves.

This is your life. Parent it.

TRY THIS: YOUR P.A.R.E.N.T. GUIDE SHEET

In the beginning, I recommend using a licensed therapist to help you through the re-parenting process. Once you feel confident with re-parenting and have built your skills with it, you can use this guide to lead you through the process whenever you feel the need.

- Step 1 – P-ause whatever you are doing.

    Stop talking. Stop doing. Stop trying to analyze the moment. Stop looking for a solution. Still yourself, instead. Consciously, take a slow, deep breath. Then another. And another. Until you feel calm. Use a breathing technique from Chapter 4 if that's helpful.

- Step 2 – A-ccept your inner-child with open arms.

    Once you feel calm, hold your hands out, palms up, and invite your inner-child to come to you. Encourage them with words such as: I will protect you. You are safe with me. It's not your fault. You're not in trouble. I am here for you.

- Step 3 – R-eside with your inner-child.

    Attune to your inner-child by further grounding yourself into the moment, so you can receive what they have to tell you. Feel the sensations in your body. Put your hands over your heart or on your belly. Feel the air going in and out of your lungs. Feel where your head, hands, legs, and feet are in space.

- Step 4 – E-xpress your inner-child's pain.

    Open yourself to whatever your inner-child has to express to you. As you receive it, breathe and note where your body holds this trauma. Where do you feel tightness, pin pricks, aches, numbness, nausea, burning, heaviness, or any prominent sensation?

- Step 5 – N-urture your inner-child.

    Put your hands on your heart and speak to your inner-child. Reassure them. Ask them how you can help. Again, use a breathing technique to help them self-regulate. Tell them you are here and they are safe. Let them know that whatever is bothering them, they don't have to figure this out alone.

- Step 6 – T-rust that your body will heal itself.

    Just as you trust your body to heal a skinned knee, trust that you and your body know how to process and heal whatever your inner-child exposes to you. What misbelief has your inner-child revealed to you? What is the truth? Say it out loud. Say it five times. Write it down in your journal. Remember it, and use it to soothe and heal this wound the next time you're triggered.

Acknowledgments

Though some would have you believe that writing is a lonely task, it takes a village to produce a book. This book is no exception, and I am grateful for the village it has brought to me.

I could not have written this book without the support of my book coach Beth Brand. She encouraged and guided me as I worked through my manuscript from organizing my ideas through writing the last chapter—and the many steps after. Beth's expertise and friendship provided those Bigger, Stronger, Wiser, & Kind hands I needed. I thank her for believing in me and this project.

Clare Finney designed the cover for this book—which makes me smile every time I look at it. Her ability to capture the heart of the text in a single image stuns me. I'm in awe of and so appreciative of her talent.

No one makes the journey from manuscript to published book easier or more pleasant than the team at Authority Publishing. I am beyond thankful for their expertise, professionalism, and attention to detail.

My beta readers are the best. Their feedback has strengthened this text. Their encouragement has kept me writing. I am forever indebted to them for the generosity they demonstrate in taking the time to read and comment on my manuscript so thoroughly.

I am also forever indebted to my clients. Their courage and bravery to go inward and re-parent themselves humbles me. I'm filled with gratitude that they allow me to witness both their pain and their healing.

My children Emma and Dustin have been a delight to parent. And as so many of the stories in this book prove, they have also been an unending source of lessons and personal growth for me.

Finally, I want to acknowledge Jim, my partner in life for thirty-eight years. His steadfast presence, constancy, and confidence in me—when I did not know how to have confidence in myself—have provided for me the foundation to become who I was meant to be and to write this book. There is nothing more profound a partner can provide, and I am especially fortunate that we are in this life together.

Notes

Introduction

ix **The Circle of Security.** Circle of Security International website. *https://www.circleofsecurityinternational.com.*

Chapter 2

16, 17 *The Lion King.* Directed by Roger Allers and Rob Minkoff (Burbank, CA: Walt Disney Pictures 1994)

20 *Encanto.* Directed by Charise Castro Smith. (Burbank, CA: Walt Disney Pictures 2021)

Chapter 3

24 **I Corinthians 13:11** (New International Version, Biblica, 1978)

25, 37 **Brainspotting.** David Grand, *Brainspotting: The Revolutionary New Therapy for Rapid and Effective Change.* (Sounds True, 2013)

37 **Eye Movement Desensitization and Reprocessing (EMDR).** Shapiro, Francine. *Eye movement desensitization and reprocessing (EMDR): Basic principles, protocols, and procedures.* (Guilford Press, 2001)

37 **Emotional Freedom Technique (EFT) or Tapping.** Nick Ortner, *The Tapping Solution: A Revolutionary System for Stress-Free Living.* (Hay House, 2014)

Chapter 4

39 **These early childhood interactions form what psychologist call our "attachment syle"...** Attachment theory has its origins

in the work of John Bowlby, though many other researchers—including Mary Ainsworth—have built on Bowlby's original ideas and added much to the theory over the years. John Bowlby, *Attachment: Attachment and Loss, Volume 1*. (Basic Books, 2nd edition, 1983)

Chapter 6

64 **The Strange Situation.** Mary D. Salter Ainsworth, and Silvia M. Bell. "Attachment, Exploration, and Separation: Illustrated by the Behavior of One-Year-Olds in a Strange Situation." *Child Development* 41, no. 1 (1970): 49–67. https://doi.org/10.2307/1127388

Chapter 7

74 **Adverse Childhood Experiences (ACE) questionnaire.** https://www.acesaware.org/wp-content/uploads/2022/07/ACE-Questionnaire-for-Adults-Identified-English-rev.7.26.22.pdf

74 **During the study, researchers asked 17,000 patients...** Vincent J. Felitti MD, FACP, Robert F Anda MD, MS, Dale Nordenberg MD, David F. Williamson MS, PhD, Alison M. Spitz MS, MPH, Valerie Edwards BA, Mary P. Koss PhD, James S. Marks MD, MPS. "Relationship of Childhood Abuse and Household Dysfunction to Many of the Leading Causes of Death in Adults. The Adverse Childhood Experience (ACE) Study." *American Journal of Preventive Medicine*. (May 1998) Vol. 14, Issue 4, 245-258. https://www.ajpmonline.org/article/S0749-3797(98)00017-8/fulltext

Chapter 8

94 *You Hurt My Feelings*. Directed by Nicole Holofcener. (FilmNation Entertainment, 2023)

95 **In her book,** *Mindset*...Carol Dweck, *Mindset: The New Psychology of Success, How We Can Learn to Fulfill Our Potential*. (Ballantine Books, Updated Edition, 2007)

www.ingramcontent.com/pod-product-compliance
Lightning Source LLC
Chambersburg PA
CBHW060504030426
42337CB00015B/1729